Stumbling in the Dark - The Dangers of Alcohol

Joshua Rhoades

Published by Joshua Paul Rhoades, 2024.

STUMBLING IN THE DARK - THE DANGERS OF ALCOHOL

First edition. September 2, 2024.

ISBN: 979-8227103055

Written by Joshua Rhoades.

Also by Joshua Rhoades

Courage Under Fire: David's Stand On The Battlefield
Jonah's Journey: Voices Of Redemption And Lessons In Obedience
The Furnace Of Faith: 12 Principles From The Heat Of Faith
Whispers of Hope: Inspiring Stories of Men's Prayers In Scripture
Frontier Legends: The Oregon Dream
Elijah: A Beacon Of Boldness
HOOK, LINE & SAVIOUR - Faith Reflections from Fishing
Driven By Faith: Motor Racing Inspired Christian Life
30 Day Devotional - Bold and Strong- Coffee Devotions for a
Courageous Christian Walk
Authentic Christianity: The Heart of Old Time Religion
Consider The Ant - God's Tiny Preachers
Flee Fornication: The Plea For Purity
Renewed Hope- How to Find Encouragement in God
Sounding The Call - The Voice of Conviction
The Altar - Where Heaven Meets Earth
The Bible's Battlefields- Timeless Lessons from Ancient Wars
The Sacred Art of Silence - How Silence Speaks in Scripture
Under Fire- The Sanctity of the Traditional Biblical Home
Who Is on the Lord's Side? A Call to Righteousness
What Is Truth? - From Skepticism to Submission
First and Goal- Faith and Football Fundamentals
From Dugout to Devotion- Spiritual Lessons from Baseball
Par for the Course- Faith and Fairways
The Believer's Pace- Tools for Running Life's Marathon

The Immutable Fortress- Security in God's Unchanging Nature
Biblical Bravery
Deer Stands and Devotions: A Hunter's Walk with God
Jesus Knows- Our Hearts, Our Responsibility
Restoration - Setting The Bone
Spiritual 911- God's Word for Life's Emergency's
The Freedom of Forgiveness
The Jezebel Effect - Ancient Manipulations Modern Lessons
The Shout That Stopped The Saviour
The Time Machine Chronicles: Old Testament Characters
Anchored In Truth Exploring The Depths of Psalm 119
Biblical Counsel on Anger
Stumbling in the Dark - The Dangers of Alcohol

Introduction

Alcohol has been a part of human culture for thousands of years, often seen as a source of celebration, relaxation, or even comfort. But beneath its allure lies a darker reality, especially when viewed through the lens of Scripture. The Bible is clear about the dangers of alcohol, warning repeatedly of the pitfalls that come with indulgence. In "Stumbling in the Dark - The Dangers of Alcohol", we explore the Bible's teachings on alcohol, uncovering the profound lessons that are as relevant today as they were in ancient times. This book looks into the ways alcohol can distort judgment, erode self-control, and lead to decisions that not only harm the individual but also those around them. From the warnings given to kings and leaders about the perils of drinking, to the tragic stories of lives unraveled by alcohol, Scripture provides a sobering view of how easily one can stumble into darkness when intoxication takes hold. Yet, these warnings are not just about avoiding alcohol—they are about understanding the deeper spiritual consequences of letting anything take control over us, leading us away from a life of clarity, purpose, and devotion to God. Alcohol, as the Bible shows us, is not merely a physical danger but a spiritual one, capable of clouding our judgment, dulling our spiritual senses, and ultimately leading us down a path of destruction. This book is a call to vigilance, encouraging readers to examine their own lives, recognize the subtle ways alcohol can take root, and make choices that align with the wisdom and guidance found in Scripture. By understanding the dangers of alcohol through the Bible's teachings, we can better navigate the challenges of life, remaining steadfast in our faith and clear in our purpose. "Stumbling in the Dark – The Dangers of Alcohol" is more than just a warning—it's an invitation to step into the light, to live a life of sobriety, both physically and spiritually, and to embrace the fullness of life that comes from walking in the wisdom of God's Word.

Chapter 1 – The Senseless

Proverbs 20:1, "Wine is a mocker, strong drink is raging: and whosoever is deceived thereby is not wise," offers a profound warning about the dangers of alcohol, painting a vivid picture of how it can lead us down a path of senseless decisions and regret. This verse encapsulates the essence of the Bible's caution against the use of alcohol, highlighting its ability to deceive and mock those who fall under its influence. The imagery of wine as a "mocker" suggests that alcohol has a way of making a fool out of those who indulge in it, leading them to believe they are in control when, in reality, they are being controlled by it. The description of strong drink as "raging" adds another layer to this warning, emphasizing the destructive power of alcohol. It is not just a mild influence; it is a force that can rage out of control, causing chaos and harm to those who underestimate its effects. The verse makes it clear that those who are deceived by alcohol are not wise, pointing to the senselessness of allowing oneself to be led astray by something so destructive.

When we consider the impact of alcohol as described in this verse, we can see how it leads to a series of poor decisions that can have long-lasting consequences. Alcohol impairs judgment, dulls the senses, and weakens the will, making it easier for individuals to make choices they would never consider in a sober state. These choices can range from reckless behavior to harmful words and actions that damage relationships and reputations. The Bible, through this verse, urges us to recognize the deceitful nature of alcohol—it presents itself as a source of pleasure or relief, but it ultimately brings pain, regret, and often shame. The mockery of wine is that it promises something good but delivers something harmful, and those who are deceived by it find themselves trapped in a cycle of bad decisions and negative outcomes.

The senselessness of alcohol consumption as depicted in Proverbs 20:1 is not just about the immediate effects of drunkenness but also about the long-term consequences that can ensue. For many, what begins as casual drinking can evolve into a dependency that takes over their lives. The verse's mention of wine as a "mocker" can be seen as a metaphor for how alcohol, when given a foothold, can mock a person's life, leading them into deeper and deeper levels of foolishness and despair. It blinds them to the reality of their situation, making them believe that they are immune to the problems that alcohol brings, even as their life begins to unravel. The raging nature of strong drink, as described in the verse, represents the uncontrollable and unpredictable effects of alcohol, which can lead to outbursts of anger, violence, and other destructive behaviors. These are the kinds of consequences that can have a devastating impact not just on the individual but also on their family, friends, and community.

Moreover, the verse calls attention to the deception that alcohol brings. It lures individuals with the promise of happiness, relaxation, or escape from life's difficulties, but these are temporary and illusory benefits that come with a heavy price. The deception of alcohol lies in its ability to convince people that they can handle it, that it will not affect them as it has affected others. This is part of the mockery that wine brings—it leads individuals to believe they are stronger or smarter than those who have fallen before them, only to bring them to the same or even worse fate. The Bible uses this verse to strip away the illusion and to reveal the truth: that those who are deceived by alcohol are not wise, but senseless, because they are allowing a substance to take control of their lives and lead them down a path of destruction.

The concept of wisdom versus senselessness is central to this verse. Wisdom, in the biblical sense, involves making decisions that are aligned with God's will and that lead to a life of peace, joy, and fulfillment. Senselessness, on the other hand, is characterized by decisions that are short-sighted, self-indulgent, and ultimately harmful. The choice to indulge in alcohol to the point of intoxication is portrayed as a senseless one because it goes against the principles of self-control, discipline, and respect for one's own body and life that are emphasized throughout Scripture. The verse suggests that wisdom lies in recognizing the dangers of alcohol and choosing to avoid its deceptive allure, rather than being drawn into its trap.

Additionally, Proverbs 20:1 serves as a cautionary tale that extends beyond just the individual. The senselessness of alcohol consumption has ripple effects that can touch many lives. Families can be torn apart by the behaviors that arise from drunkenness, friendships can be destroyed, and careers can be derailed. The societal impact of alcohol is also significant, contributing to accidents, crimes, and a host of other problems. By describing wine as a mocker and strong drink as raging, the Bible underscores the idea that the consequences of alcohol extend far beyond the individual and can lead to widespread harm. It's a reminder that the decisions we make, particularly those influenced by alcohol, do not exist in a vacuum but have the potential to affect many others.

Furthermore, the verse challenges us to consider the spiritual implications of alcohol use. In the context of biblical teaching, allowing something like alcohol to have control over us is seen as contrary to the life that God calls us to live. We are urged to be sober-minded, to live lives that are guided by the Holy Spirit rather than by substances that cloud our judgment and lead us away from God's will. The wisdom that Proverbs 20:1 advocates for is one that prioritizes spiritual clarity and strength over temporary and destructive pleasures. By avoiding the deception of alcohol, we are better able to hear God's voice, to follow His guidance, and to live in a way that reflects His love and wisdom.

In conclusion, Proverbs 20:1 offers a compelling and sobering warning about the dangers of alcohol, portraying it as a mocker that deceives and a raging force that leads to senselessness. The verse calls us to recognize the destructive power of alcohol and to make wise choices that align with God's will. It reminds us that wisdom lies in avoiding the traps that alcohol sets, and in choosing a path that leads to life, peace, and spiritual fulfillment. The senselessness of alcohol consumption, as depicted in this verse, serves as a powerful reminder of the importance of self-control, discipline, and a commitment to living a life that honors God and protects not just ourselves, but those around us. By heeding the warning of Proverbs 20:1, we can avoid the mockery and destruction that alcohol brings and instead embrace a life of wisdom, clarity, and true joy.

Chapter 2 – The Shame

Habakkuk 2:15, "Woe unto him that giveth his neighbour drink, that puttest thy bottle to him, and makest him drunken also, that thou mayest look on their nakedness!" offers a stern warning about the dangers and shame associated with alcohol, particularly when it is used to manipulate or harm others. This verse vividly illustrates the dark side of alcohol, not just in its ability to impair judgment and lead to personal downfall, but also in how it can be used as a tool for exploitation and abuse. The verse begins with a pronouncement of "woe," a word that signals deep sorrow, regret, and impending judgment. It is directed at those who use alcohol to take advantage of others, highlighting the shameful and disgraceful nature of such actions. In ancient times, as in many cultures today, hospitality and the sharing of drinks were common social practices, but this verse exposes the sinister twist when someone deliberately gets another person drunk with the intention of humiliating or exploiting them.

The mention of "looking on their nakedness" is particularly striking, as it symbolizes the stripping away of dignity and the exposure of vulnerability. In this context, alcohol becomes a weapon that leads to the degradation and shaming of another person. This is not just a private matter of personal moral failing; it's a profound violation of trust and human decency. The Bible here is clear: there is a deep moral and spiritual darkness associated with leading someone into drunkenness for the purpose of shaming or exploiting them. The act of giving someone a drink to make them drunk so that they can be taken advantage of is one of the most deplorable forms of betrayal, and it brings disgrace not only to the victim but also to the perpetrator. The verse condemns this behavior in the strongest terms, warning that such actions will not go unnoticed by God and that those who engage in them will face His judgment.

This verse also brings to light the broader implications of alcohol use within society, particularly how it can be abused to harm others. The scenario depicted in Habakkuk 2:15 is not just about an isolated incident, but rather a reflection of the broader dangers of alcohol when it is used irresponsibly or maliciously. Alcohol has the power to lower inhibitions and impair judgment, making individuals more susceptible to manipulation and harm. When someone intentionally uses alcohol to bring about this state in another person, they are not only taking advantage of their physical and mental vulnerability but also committing a grave sin against that person's dignity and humanity. The shame that results from such actions is profound, affecting both the victim and the perpetrator. For the victim, there is the shame of being exposed and humiliated, often leading to long-lasting emotional and psychological scars. For the perpetrator, there is the shame of having committed an act so deeply rooted in selfishness and malice that it corrupts their own soul and leads them away from the path of righteousness.

Moreover, Habakkuk 2:15 speaks to the issue of accountability and the moral responsibility we have toward others, especially in how we influence and treat them. The verse condemns those who use alcohol to lead others into sin, highlighting the seriousness of causing another person to stumble. This is not just a matter of individual morality but of communal ethics—how our actions impact those around us. The Bible consistently teaches that we are our brother's keeper, meaning we have a responsibility to look out for the well-being of others, not to lead them into harm or disgrace. When someone uses alcohol to take advantage of another, they are betraying that responsibility and bringing shame upon themselves. The verse serves as a powerful reminder that our actions have consequences, not just for ourselves but for others, and that we must be mindful of how we use the influence we have, particularly when it involves something as potentially dangerous as alcohol.

The shame and disgrace highlighted in this verse are also a reflection of the broader societal and cultural issues surrounding alcohol use and abuse. Throughout history, alcohol has been associated with both social bonding and social decay. It has the power to bring people together in celebration, but it also has the potential to tear them apart when misused. Habakkuk 2:15 warns against the darker side of this duality, where alcohol is used not for fellowship or joy, but for exploitation and harm. The verse paints a picture of a society where trust is eroded, and relationships are corrupted by the misuse of alcohol, leading to a culture of shame and dishonor. This serves as a cautionary tale, urging us to consider the broader implications of our actions and the role that alcohol plays in our lives and communities.

Furthermore, the verse invites us to reflect on the nature of shame itself and how it can be both a consequence and a tool of control. In the context of Habakkuk 2:15, shame is the intended outcome of the perpetrator's actions—they want to strip away the victim's dignity and leave them exposed and humiliated. But in doing so, they also bring shame upon themselves, as they reveal their own moral bankruptcy and willingness to harm others for their own gain. This creates a cycle of shame that spreads from the individual to the community, affecting everyone involved. The Bible warns us against falling into this cycle, urging us to act with integrity and compassion rather than giving in to the temptations of power and control that alcohol can exacerbate.

In conclusion, Habakkuk 2:15 offers a stark warning about the dangers of alcohol, particularly when it is used to lead others into shame and disgrace. The verse condemns those who exploit the vulnerability of others through drunkenness, highlighting the deep moral and spiritual corruption involved in such actions. It calls us to be mindful of how we use alcohol and to recognize the profound responsibility we have to protect and uplift those around us, rather than leading them into harm. The shame that results from the misuse of alcohol is not limited to the victim; it spreads to the perpetrator and the broader community, creating a culture of dishonor and broken trust. By reflecting on this verse, we are reminded of the importance of treating others with respect and dignity, and of the dangers that come when we use alcohol to manipulate or harm. This verse serves as a powerful reminder that true wisdom and righteousness lie in building others up, not tearing them down, and that we must be ever vigilant in avoiding the senseless and shameful paths that alcohol can lead us down.

Chapter 3 – The Snake-like

Proverbs 23:31-32, "Look not thou upon the wine when it is red, when it giveth his colour in the cup, when it moveth itself aright. At the last it biteth like a serpent, and stingeth like an adder," presents a vivid and powerful image of the dangers of alcohol, warning us of its snake-like consequences. The verse paints a picture of wine as something deceptively attractive, almost hypnotic in its allure. The rich, red color of the wine and the way it swirls in the cup are described in a way that highlights its appeal, drawing in those who gaze upon it. This imagery taps into the sensory appeal of alcohol, which can be enticing and seem harmless or even desirable at first glance. The Bible, however, warns that beneath this attractive surface lies a hidden danger, much like the serpent in the Garden of Eden, whose appearance was appealing, yet whose bite brought about profound consequences.

The comparison to a serpent or an adder—a poisonous snake—underscores the treacherous nature of alcohol. It suggests that alcohol, much like a snake, can strike unexpectedly and with harmful effects. The bite of a serpent is often sudden and painful, bringing poison into the body that can spread and cause significant damage. In the same way, the initial pleasure or relief that alcohol might offer can quickly turn into something dangerous, leading to pain, regret, and destruction. The verse is a stark reminder that alcohol, though it may seem harmless or even beneficial in moderation, has the potential to lead us down a path of harm if we are not careful. The description of alcohol as something that "biteth like a serpent" and "stingeth like an adder" is meant to evoke a sense of caution, warning us not to be deceived by its initial allure.

The snake-like nature of alcohol's consequences is particularly relevant when we consider how alcohol can affect our lives in both the short and long term. In the short term, alcohol can impair judgment, leading to decisions and actions that we might later regret. It can cause us to say things we don't mean, to act in ways that are out of character, or to engage in risky behaviors that we would normally avoid. Just as a snake's bite delivers venom that quickly spreads through the body, alcohol's effects can rapidly take hold, leading to a cascade of negative consequences. In the long term, the damage caused by alcohol can be even more profound. Addiction, broken relationships, financial problems, health issues, and spiritual decline are just a few of the potential outcomes of allowing alcohol to take control of our lives. The Bible's warning in Proverbs 23:31-32 is not just about the immediate effects of drinking, but about the far-reaching consequences that can follow.

One of the most dangerous aspects of alcohol, as highlighted in this verse, is its deceptive nature. The initial experience of drinking—whether it's the taste, the relaxation, or the social aspect—can mask the dangers that lie beneath the surface. The Bible warns us not to be fooled by the superficial appeal of alcohol, much like we should not be fooled by the beauty of a snake's skin. The danger is real, even if it's not immediately apparent. This deception is what makes alcohol so insidious; it can lure people in with promises of pleasure, escape, or social acceptance, but it ultimately delivers pain, regret, and sometimes even destruction. The verse urges us to be aware of this deception, to recognize that what seems harmless or appealing can have serious and harmful consequences.

Furthermore, the snake-like consequences of alcohol are not just physical but also spiritual. Alcohol can dull our senses, not just physically but spiritually, making it harder for us to connect with God and to live according to His will. Just as a snake's venom can cause paralysis or death, alcohol can paralyze our spiritual growth and lead us away from the path that God has set for us. It can create a barrier between us and God, making it difficult to hear His voice, to feel His presence, or to follow His guidance. The Bible's warning in Proverbs 23:31-32 is a call to be vigilant, to recognize the dangers that alcohol poses not just to our bodies and minds, but to our souls as well. It's a reminder that we need to stay spiritually awake and alert, and not let alcohol or any other substance dull our connection to God.

The comparison to a serpent also brings to mind the idea of temptation and the consequences of giving in to it. In the Garden of Eden, the serpent tempted Eve with something that seemed desirable and harmless, but that ultimately led to the fall of humanity. In the same way, alcohol can be a temptation that seems harmless at first, but that can lead to serious consequences. The Bible's warning is clear: don't be deceived by the initial appeal, because the end result can be much more harmful than you might expect. This is a powerful reminder of the importance of self-control and discernment. We need to be able to recognize when something that seems good or harmless might actually be leading us down a dangerous path. The ability to resist temptation, to see through the deception, is a key part of living a life that is aligned with God's will.

Moreover, the snake-like consequences of alcohol can also be seen in the way it can trap us in a cycle of dependency and addiction. Just as a snake can ensnare its prey, alcohol can ensnare those who become dependent on it, leading them into a cycle of use and abuse that can be incredibly difficult to break. The initial allure of alcohol can lead to a gradual increase in use, as the person seeks to recapture the pleasure or escape that they experienced the first time. Over time, this can develop into a dependency, where the person feels they need alcohol to function, to cope, or to feel normal. The verse's warning about the snake-like nature of alcohol is particularly relevant here, as it highlights the way that alcohol can slowly tighten its grip on a person's life, leading them further and further away from the life that God wants for them.

In conclusion, Proverbs 23:31-32 offers a compelling and vivid warning about the dangers of alcohol, comparing its effects to the bite of a serpent and the sting of an adder. The verse urges us not to be deceived by the initial allure of alcohol, warning that its consequences can be as painful and destructive as a snake's bite. The snake-like nature of alcohol's consequences is seen in the way it can impair judgment, lead to harmful decisions, and create long-term damage in our lives. It also highlights the spiritual dangers of alcohol, warning us not to let it dull our connection to God or lead us away from His path. The Bible's warning in this verse is a call to vigilance, to recognize the dangers that lie beneath the surface, and to avoid the deception that alcohol can bring. By heeding this warning, we can protect ourselves from the snake-like consequences of alcohol, and live a life that is aligned with God's will, free from the traps and dangers that alcohol can bring.

Chapter 4 – The Self-destructive

Isaiah 5:11, "Woe unto them that rise up early in the morning, that they may follow strong drink; that continue until night, till wine inflame them!" provides a stark and sobering warning about the self-destructive nature of a life consumed by alcohol. This verse paints a picture of individuals who have allowed alcohol to dominate their lives to the point where it dictates their daily routine. The phrase "rise up early in the morning" suggests that these individuals prioritize alcohol above all else, starting their day with a drink and continuing throughout the night until they are inflamed by wine. The use of the word "inflame" is particularly powerful, evoking an image of burning or raging out of control, much like a fire that consumes everything in its path. This imagery is fitting for the destructive power of alcohol, which, when abused, can lead to a life that spirals out of control, bringing with it a host of negative consequences that affect not only the individual but also those around them.

The verse begins with a pronouncement of "woe," a term often used in the Bible to express deep sorrow, regret, or condemnation. This "woe" is directed at those who have allowed their lives to be dominated by alcohol, to the point where it has become the central focus of their existence. The warning here is clear: a life consumed by alcohol is a life on a path to destruction. The self-destructive behavior described in this verse is not just about the physical effects of alcohol, such as health problems or addiction, but also about the spiritual and moral decay that accompanies a life inflamed by alcohol. When alcohol takes over, it dulls the senses, impairs judgment, and weakens the will, making it difficult for individuals to make wise decisions or to live in accordance with their values and beliefs. Over time, this leads to a downward spiral where the individual becomes more and more consumed by alcohol, losing sight of what truly matters in life.

The self-destructive nature of alcohol is evident in the way it affects all aspects of a person's life. Physically, alcohol can take a severe toll on the body, leading to a range of health problems, including liver disease, heart problems, and neurological damage. These health issues are often compounded by the fact that individuals who are addicted to alcohol may neglect their overall health, skipping meals, failing to exercise, and ignoring medical advice. The phrase "till wine inflame them" suggests that this is not just a momentary lapse in judgment, but a continuous, ongoing pattern of behavior that ultimately consumes the individual. The physical consequences of such a lifestyle are devastating, often leading to chronic illness, disability, or even premature death.

In addition to the physical toll, the self-destructive behavior described in Isaiah 5:11 also has profound emotional and psychological effects. Alcohol, when abused, can exacerbate feelings of depression, anxiety, and hopelessness, creating a vicious cycle where the individual drinks to escape their negative emotions, only to find that alcohol intensifies those feelings in the long run. The phrase "rise up early in the morning" suggests that these individuals are using alcohol as a way to cope with their problems, starting their day with a drink in an attempt to numb their pain or escape from reality. However, rather than providing relief, this reliance on alcohol only deepens their emotional and psychological distress, leading to a life marked by constant struggle and suffering.

The self-destructive behavior associated with alcohol also extends to an individual's relationships. Alcohol abuse can strain relationships with family, friends, and colleagues, leading to conflicts, misunderstandings, and broken bonds. The verse describes a life where alcohol takes precedence over all else, suggesting that these individuals may neglect their responsibilities and obligations to others in favor of their drinking habits. This neglect can cause significant harm to relationships, as loved ones feel abandoned, hurt, or betrayed by the individual's actions. Over time, this can lead to isolation and loneliness, as the individual pushes away those who care about them in favor of their addiction. The self-destructive nature of alcohol is evident in the way it destroys relationships, leaving the individual alone and disconnected from the support and love they need to thrive.

Moreover, the spiritual consequences of a life inflamed by alcohol are perhaps the most profound. The Bible consistently teaches that we are called to live lives of purpose, meaning, and righteousness, following God's will and seeking to grow in our relationship with Him. However, when alcohol takes over, it can lead to a spiritual decline, as individuals become more focused on their own desires and pleasures than on their relationship with God. The verse's warning of "woe" is a reminder that a life dominated by alcohol is a life that is moving away from God's plan and purpose. The self-destructive behavior described in Isaiah 5:11 is not just about the physical and emotional toll of alcohol, but also about the spiritual damage that occurs when we allow alcohol to take control of our lives.

The phrase "till wine inflame them" also suggests a loss of self-control, as individuals become consumed by their desire for alcohol, unable to resist its pull. This loss of control is a hallmark of addiction, where the individual becomes enslaved to their substance of choice, losing the ability to make rational decisions or to prioritize their health, relationships, and spiritual well-being. The self-destructive behavior described in this verse is a result of this loss of control, as individuals become trapped in a cycle of addiction that leads them further and further away from the life that God intends for them. The Bible's warning in Isaiah 5:11 is a call to recognize the dangers of alcohol and to avoid the self-destructive path that it can lead to.

In addition to the personal consequences, the self-destructive behavior associated with alcohol also has broader societal implications. Alcohol abuse is a leading cause of accidents, injuries, and violence, contributing to a range of social problems that affect individuals, families, and communities. The verse's depiction of individuals who "rise up early in the morning" to follow strong drink suggests that this behavior is not just a personal issue, but a societal one, as the effects of alcohol abuse ripple out to affect everyone around the individual. The self-destructive nature of alcohol is evident in the way it contributes to social decay, leading to increased crime, poverty, and suffering in communities. The Bible's warning in Isaiah 5:11 is a reminder that the consequences of alcohol abuse are not limited to the individual, but have far-reaching effects that can harm society as a whole.

The self-destructive behavior described in Isaiah 5:11 is a powerful reminder of the importance of self-control and moderation. The Bible consistently teaches that we are to be good stewards of our bodies, minds, and souls, taking care of ourselves and living in a way that honors God. When we allow alcohol to take control of our lives, we are failing in this responsibility, choosing instead to indulge in behavior that leads to destruction. The verse's warning of "woe" is a call to turn away from this path and to seek a life of moderation, self-control, and spiritual growth. The self-destructive nature of alcohol is a reminder that we must be vigilant in guarding against the temptations that can lead us away from God's will.

In conclusion, Isaiah 5:11 offers a compelling and sobering warning about the self-destructive nature of a life inflamed by alcohol. The verse paints a vivid picture of individuals who have allowed alcohol to dominate their lives, leading to a downward spiral of physical, emotional, and spiritual decline. The self-destructive behavior described in this verse is a result of the loss of self-control that comes with addiction, as individuals become consumed by their desire for alcohol and lose sight of what truly matters in life. The Bible's warning in Isaiah 5:11 is a call to recognize the dangers of alcohol and to avoid the self-destructive path that it can lead to. By heeding this warning, we can protect ourselves from the physical, emotional, and spiritual damage that alcohol can cause, and live lives that are aligned with God's will, filled with purpose, meaning, and true fulfillment. The self-destructive nature of alcohol is a reminder that we must be vigilant in guarding against the temptations that can lead us away from the life that God intends for us. By choosing a life of moderation, self-control, and spiritual growth, we can avoid the woe that comes with a life inflamed by alcohol, and instead live in the peace and joy that God desires for us.

Chapter 5 – The Skewed

Proverbs 31:4-5, "It is not for kings, O Lemuel, it is not for kings to drink wine; nor for princes strong drink: Lest they drink, and forget the law, and pervert the judgment of any of the afflicted," offers a powerful warning about the dangers of alcohol, particularly for those in positions of authority and responsibility. This verse, spoken by King Lemuel's mother, highlights the critical role that clear, sober judgment plays in leadership and decision-making. The instruction is straightforward: those who are entrusted with the welfare of others—kings, princes, leaders—should avoid alcohol because of its potential to skew their judgment. The stakes are high when it comes to leadership, and the ability to make fair, wise, and just decisions is paramount. When alcohol enters the picture, it clouds the mind, dulls the senses, and leads to impaired decision-making, which can have serious consequences, not just for the individual but for those they lead and serve.

The idea of "skewed" judgment is central to this passage. To skew something means to distort or twist it out of its true or natural state, and this is precisely what alcohol does to our judgment. In the context of leadership, where decisions can impact the lives of many, the distortion of judgment can lead to injustice, unfairness, and harm. A leader who drinks and allows their judgment to be skewed may forget the laws and principles they are supposed to uphold. They might make decisions based on their altered state of mind, rather than on reason, morality, or the well-being of their people. The verse warns that such a leader might "forget the law," indicating a lapse in memory, responsibility, and adherence to what is right. This forgetting is not just about failing to recall facts or rules, but about neglecting the very essence of justice and fairness, which are the cornerstones of good leadership.

Moreover, the passage points out that alcohol can lead to the perversion of judgment, particularly when it comes to the "afflicted."

In biblical terms, the afflicted often refer to those who are vulnerable, oppressed, or in need of justice. These are the individuals who rely on their leaders to protect their rights, to ensure they are treated fairly, and to see that justice is done. When a leader's judgment is skewed by alcohol, they are more likely to make decisions that harm these vulnerable individuals. They might side with the powerful against the weak, ignore the cries of those in need, or even actively participate in injustice. The perversion of judgment is one of the most dangerous consequences of alcohol, as it can lead to a complete reversal of what is right and just. Instead of upholding the law and protecting the afflicted, a leader under the influence of alcohol might do the exact opposite, causing great harm to those who depend on them.

The danger of skewed judgment due to alcohol is not limited to kings and princes; it applies to anyone in a position of responsibility or influence. Whether in government, business, family, or community, those who are looked to for guidance and decision-making must be able to think clearly and act justly. Alcohol undermines this ability, leading to poor decisions that can have far-reaching consequences. In a family, a parent who drinks excessively might make choices that negatively affect their children, such as neglecting their needs, exposing them to harmful situations, or setting a bad example. In a business, a manager who drinks might fail to make sound financial decisions, leading to losses or even the collapse of the company. In government, a lawmaker or judge under the influence might pass laws or make rulings that are unjust, harming individuals and society as a whole. The skewing of judgment by alcohol is a threat to the integrity and effectiveness of leadership at all levels.

Furthermore, the verse underscores the importance of self-control and discipline in leadership. To abstain from alcohol, especially in cultures where drinking might be common or even expected, requires a commitment to prioritizing the well-being of others above personal pleasure. Leaders who exercise this discipline demonstrate that they are serious about their responsibilities and that they are committed to making decisions that are in the best interest of those they serve. The Bible often highlights self-control as a virtue, and in this context, it is closely tied to wisdom and effective leadership. By avoiding alcohol, leaders can ensure that their judgment remains unclouded, their decisions remain fair, and their actions remain just. This self-discipline is not just about abstaining from a substance; it is about maintaining the clarity of mind and moral integrity needed to lead effectively.

The skewing of judgment by alcohol also speaks to the broader theme of the consequences of indulgence. Throughout Scripture, there is a recurring emphasis on the dangers of overindulgence, whether in food, drink, or other pleasures. These warnings are not just about the physical effects of excess, but about the spiritual and moral dangers that come with allowing desires to control one's actions. Alcohol, in particular, is often singled out because of its powerful ability to impair judgment and lead to behavior that is out of character, irresponsible, or even harmful. The verse from Proverbs 31:4-5 serves as a reminder that indulgence in alcohol can lead to a loss of control, resulting in decisions that are not only unwise but also unjust. The skewing of judgment is a natural consequence of letting indulgence take the place of discipline and responsibility.

The imagery in Proverbs 31:4-5 also invites reflection on the broader societal implications of alcohol use among leaders. When those in power are influenced by alcohol, the ripple effects can be profound. Laws may be passed that do not reflect the needs or rights of the people, justice may be denied to those who most need it, and the overall moral fabric of society may begin to unravel. The verse's emphasis on the dangers of alcohol for kings and princes highlights the importance of sober, clear-headed leadership in maintaining a just and orderly society. When leaders fail to uphold this standard, the consequences can be widespread, affecting not just individuals but entire communities and nations. The skewing of judgment by alcohol is not just a personal failing; it is a societal risk that can lead to the erosion of justice, fairness, and integrity at all levels of governance.

Additionally, the verse from Proverbs 31:4-5 can be seen as a call to all individuals, not just leaders, to be mindful of the influence of alcohol in their lives. While the direct warning is to kings and princes, the underlying principle applies to everyone. Each person has a sphere of influence, whether in their family, workplace, or community, and the decisions they make can impact others. The skewing of judgment by alcohol can lead to actions that harm not only oneself but also those around them. By recognizing the potential for alcohol to distort judgment, individuals can make more informed choices about their drinking habits, understanding that the consequences extend beyond their own lives. The Bible's warning is a call to sobriety in all aspects of life, encouraging people to prioritize clear thinking, wise decision-making, and the well-being of others.

Moreover, Proverbs 31:4-5 serves as a reminder of the broader biblical theme of the importance of wisdom in leadership. Throughout the Bible, wisdom is portrayed as a vital quality for anyone in a position of authority. Wisdom involves not just knowledge and understanding, but also the ability to make sound decisions that are in alignment with God's will and the principles of justice and righteousness. Alcohol, by skewing judgment, undermines this wisdom, leading to decisions that are not based on truth, fairness, or the greater good. The verse warns that when leaders allow alcohol to influence their decisions, they are at risk of forsaking wisdom and, as a result, failing in their responsibilities. This is a serious danger, as the consequences of unwise leadership can be devastating for those who depend on them for guidance, protection, and justice.

In conclusion, Proverbs 31:4-5 offers a compelling and cautionary message about the dangers of alcohol, particularly for those in positions of leadership. The verse highlights the risk of skewed judgment that comes with drinking, warning that alcohol can lead to a forgetting of the law and a perversion of justice. This warning is relevant not just for kings and princes, but for anyone who holds responsibility or influence over others. The skewing of judgment by alcohol is a threat to the integrity and effectiveness of leadership, leading to decisions that can harm individuals, communities, and society as a whole. The Bible's message is clear: sobriety and self-control are essential for those who wish to lead with wisdom, fairness, and justice. By avoiding the dangers of alcohol, leaders can ensure that their judgment remains clear, their decisions remain just, and their actions remain aligned with the principles of righteousness and the well-being of those they serve. The skewing of judgment by alcohol is a powerful reminder of the importance of maintaining clarity of mind and moral integrity in all aspects of life, particularly in leadership, where the consequences of poor decisions can have far-reaching effects.

Chapter 6 – The Squandered

Ephesians 5:18, "And be not drunk with wine, wherein is excess; but be filled with the Spirit," provides a profound and clear warning about the dangers of alcohol, particularly the way it leads to squandered opportunities, wasted potential, and lives that drift away from the purpose and fulfillment that God intends for us. The verse presents a stark contrast between two paths: one marked by excess and indulgence in wine, and the other filled with the Spirit, a life enriched by God's presence and purpose. The use of the word "excess" in relation to wine captures the idea of going beyond healthy or moderate limits, diving into a state where control is lost, and with it, the clarity of mind and purpose. This excess is not just about drinking too much, but about what is lost in the process—the opportunities, the potential, the meaningful life that could have been. When Paul warns against being drunk with wine, he is addressing more than just the physical act of drinking; he is cautioning against the larger danger of allowing any substance or behavior to take control of our lives, leading us to squander the gifts, talents, and opportunities that God has given us.

The concept of "squandered" opportunities is central to this verse. To squander something means to waste it thoughtlessly, to let it slip away without taking advantage of it or appreciating its value. In the context of Ephesians 5:18, the excess of wine leads to a life where opportunities are missed, and the potential is not realized. This can happen in many ways: a person who is drunk or habitually overindulges in alcohol may miss out on career advancements, fail to nurture important relationships, or neglect personal growth and spiritual development. Alcohol, when consumed in excess, has a way of dulling the senses, numbing the mind, and creating a false sense of contentment that keeps a person from pursuing their true calling or fulfilling their potential. The temporary pleasure or escape that alcohol provides can deceive a person into thinking that everything is fine, when in reality, they are letting precious time and opportunities pass them by. The Bible's warning here is not just about the dangers of alcohol itself, but about the larger consequences of living a life that is marked by excess and indulgence, rather than discipline, purpose, and a connection to the Spirit.

The idea of a life "filled with the Spirit" serves as a powerful counterpoint to the dangers of excess wine. While excess wine leads to squandered opportunities, a life filled with the Spirit leads to growth, fulfillment, and the realization of one's true potential. Being filled with the Spirit means being guided by God, living in alignment with His will, and allowing His presence to influence every aspect of one's life. This is the life that God desires for us—a life where we are fully engaged, fully aware, and fully committed to living out our purpose. When we are filled with the Spirit, we are more likely to recognize and seize the opportunities that come our way, to build strong and meaningful relationships, and to grow in our understanding of who we are and what we are meant to do. The contrast between these two paths—one of excess and squandering, the other of spiritual fullness and purpose—is stark and serves as a reminder of the importance of making wise choices in how we live our lives.

The dangers of excess wine, as highlighted in Ephesians 5:18, are not limited to missed opportunities and wasted potential; they also include the broader impact on one's character and integrity. When a person is drunk, they are not in control of their actions, thoughts, or decisions. This lack of control can lead to behavior that is out of alignment with their values, causing harm to themselves and others. The Bible often emphasizes the importance of self-control, discipline, and living a life that reflects the character of Christ. Excess wine undermines these qualities, leading to decisions and actions that can have long-lasting negative consequences. A person who is drunk may say or do things that they would never do when sober, leading to broken relationships, damaged reputations, and a loss of trust. The verse's warning about excess wine is a call to protect one's integrity, to maintain control over one's actions, and to live in a way that honors God and reflects His love and righteousness.

In addition to the personal consequences, the dangers of excess wine extend to the impact it can have on one's family, community, and society. A person who is habitually drunk is often unable to fulfill their responsibilities to their family, whether as a parent, spouse, or caregiver. This can lead to neglect, emotional harm, and a breakdown in family relationships. Children who grow up in homes where alcohol abuse is present are often at risk for a range of negative outcomes, including emotional and behavioral problems, academic struggles, and an increased likelihood of developing substance abuse issues themselves. The impact of excess wine is not limited to the individual; it can ripple out to affect everyone around them, causing harm that can last for generations. The Bible's warning in Ephesians 5:18 is a call to consider the broader impact of one's choices, to recognize that excess and indulgence in wine can lead to a legacy of pain and loss, rather than one of love, stability, and spiritual growth.

Moreover, the dangers of excess wine as described in Ephesians 5:18 are closely tied to the idea of spiritual emptiness. When a person turns to alcohol in excess, they are often seeking to fill a void, to escape from pain, stress, or a sense of purposelessness. However, the relief that alcohol provides is temporary and ultimately unfulfilling. Rather than filling the void, excess wine only deepens it, leading to a cycle of dependency and despair. In contrast, being filled with the Spirit offers true fulfillment, a deep and lasting sense of purpose, and a connection to something greater than oneself. The Bible's message is clear: the only way to truly fill the void and find lasting fulfillment is through a relationship with God, not through the temporary and destructive escape that alcohol provides. The warning against excess wine is a call to seek spiritual fulfillment, to allow the Spirit to fill and guide one's life, rather than turning to substances that ultimately lead to emptiness and despair.

The concept of squandered lives and opportunities in Ephesians 5:18 also serves as a reminder of the brevity and preciousness of life. The Bible often speaks of life as a gift from God, one that is meant to be lived fully and with purpose. When a person allows alcohol to take control, they are essentially squandering this gift, wasting the time, talents, and opportunities that God has given them. The verse's warning against excess wine is a call to live intentionally, to make the most of the time we have, and to pursue the things that truly matter. It is a reminder that life is too short to waste on things that do not bring true fulfillment or contribute to the growth and well-being of ourselves and others. The contrast between a life of excess and a life filled with the Spirit is a powerful one, highlighting the importance of making choices that lead to a life well-lived, one that honors God and leaves a positive impact on the world.

Furthermore, Ephesians 5:18 highlights the importance of community and the role that others can play in helping us avoid the dangers of excess wine. The Bible often speaks of the importance of fellowship, accountability, and mutual support among believers. When we are part of a community that encourages us to live in alignment with God's will, we are less likely to fall into patterns of excess and indulgence. In contrast, when we are isolated or surrounded by influences that encourage excessive drinking, we are more vulnerable to falling into those patterns ourselves. The verse's warning against excess wine is also a call to surround ourselves with people who will support and encourage us in our spiritual journey, helping us to stay focused on the things that truly matter and to avoid the pitfalls of excess and indulgence.

In conclusion, Ephesians 5:18 offers a powerful and compelling warning about the dangers of excess wine, particularly the way it leads to squandered opportunities, wasted potential, and lives that drift away from the purpose and fulfillment that God intends for us. The verse contrasts the path of excess and indulgence with a life filled with the Spirit, highlighting the importance of making wise choices that lead to a life of purpose, meaning, and spiritual fulfillment. The dangers of excess wine extend beyond the individual, affecting one's character, relationships, and broader community. The Bible's message is clear: we are called to live intentionally, to make the most of the time and opportunities we have, and to seek fulfillment through a relationship with God rather than through temporary and destructive substances. The warning against excess wine is a call to live a life that honors God, protects our integrity, and leaves a positive impact on the world. By heeding this warning and choosing to be filled with the Spirit, we can avoid the dangers of squandered lives and opportunities and live a life that is truly fulfilling and aligned with God's will.

Chapter 7 – The Stumbling

Isaiah 28:7, "But they also have erred through wine, and through strong drink are out of the way; the priest and the prophet have erred through strong drink, they are swallowed up of wine, they are out of the way through strong drink; they err in vision, they stumble in judgment," provides a sobering and powerful illustration of the dangers of alcohol, particularly its ability to cause people to stumble in judgment. The verse specifically highlights how even those in positions of spiritual leadership—priests and prophets—can fall victim to the destructive power of alcohol. These leaders, who are supposed to be the moral and spiritual guides for others, are shown to have "erred through wine" and "stumbled in judgment" because of their consumption of strong drink. The use of the word "stumble" in this context is not merely physical; it represents a deeper spiritual and moral failing, a loss of clarity, and a deviation from the path of righteousness. This verse warns of the far-reaching consequences of alcohol, showing how it can lead even the wisest and most respected individuals to make poor decisions, lose their way, and ultimately fail in their responsibilities.

The concept of "stumbling" is crucial here because it conveys the idea of losing one's footing, both literally and metaphorically. In life, we all encounter obstacles and challenges that require careful navigation, and the ability to make sound decisions is essential for overcoming these hurdles. However, when alcohol is introduced, it can distort perception, impair judgment, and lead to a series of missteps. For spiritual leaders, whose role is to guide and protect their communities, stumbling in judgment can have disastrous effects, not only on their own lives but also on the lives of those who depend on them for guidance and direction. Isaiah 28:7 paints a picture of leaders who are "swallowed up of wine," meaning they have been completely consumed by their indulgence, to the point where it clouds their vision and leads them astray. This image is particularly poignant because it shows how alcohol can take over a person's life, leading them down a path of destruction and causing them to lose sight of their responsibilities and purpose.

The verse's reference to "erring in vision" highlights another critical danger of alcohol: its ability to distort reality. When a person is under the influence of alcohol, their perception of the world around them is altered. What might seem like a good idea in the moment can turn out to be a terrible decision upon sober reflection. This altered state of mind can lead to a chain of poor choices, each one compounding the previous mistake, ultimately resulting in serious consequences. For priests and prophets, whose role is to interpret and convey the will of God, this distortion of vision is particularly dangerous. Their ability to see clearly, both literally and figuratively, is essential for fulfilling their duties. When alcohol interferes with this vision, it not only affects their personal lives but also their ability to lead others. The verse suggests that when leaders stumble in their judgment due to alcohol, the entire community suffers as a result, as the guidance and wisdom they rely on become tainted and unreliable.

Moreover, the phrase "out of the way" underscores the idea that alcohol can lead individuals off the path of righteousness. The "way" in biblical terms often refers to the path that God has laid out for His people, a path of obedience, wisdom, and moral integrity. When someone is "out of the way," it means they have deviated from this path, losing their direction and purpose. Alcohol, with its ability to impair judgment and cloud the mind, is depicted as a significant factor that can cause even the most devout individuals to stray. This straying is not just a minor detour; it represents a fundamental shift away from the values and principles that are supposed to guide one's life. For leaders, being "out of the way" means they can no longer effectively guide others, as they themselves are lost and directionless. The dangers of alcohol, as highlighted in Isaiah 28:7, are thus not limited to the individual but extend to the broader community, which relies on its leaders to stay on the right path.

The idea of being "swallowed up of wine" is also significant because it conveys the notion of being consumed or overwhelmed by alcohol. This consumption is both literal and figurative—alcohol can take over a person's life, dominating their thoughts, actions, and decisions. When someone is "swallowed up," they are no longer in control; instead, they are at the mercy of their substance of choice. This lack of control is a key aspect of the "stumbling" that Isaiah 28:7 warns against. When alcohol takes over, it leads to a loss of autonomy, making it difficult for individuals to make rational decisions or to exercise the self-discipline needed to stay on the right path. This loss of control is particularly dangerous for those in leadership positions, as their decisions have far-reaching implications. A leader who is "swallowed up" by alcohol is not only failing themselves but also failing those who look to them for guidance and support.

The dangers of alcohol, as outlined in Isaiah 28:7, are not just about the immediate effects of drinking but also about the long-term consequences. When someone consistently turns to alcohol, they are setting themselves up for a pattern of poor judgment and decision-making that can have lasting effects. Over time, these missteps can accumulate, leading to a downward spiral that is difficult to reverse. The verse's warning about "erring in vision" and "stumbling in judgment" is a reminder that the consequences of alcohol abuse are not always immediate but can unfold over time, as the effects of poor decisions compound and lead to further errors and misjudgments. This is particularly true for those in positions of authority, where a single bad decision can have a domino effect, leading to a series of negative outcomes that affect not only the leader but also those they lead.

In addition to the personal and communal consequences, Isaiah 28:7 also highlights the spiritual dangers of alcohol. When someone is "out of the way" due to alcohol, they are not just lost in a physical or moral sense; they are also spiritually adrift. The Bible consistently teaches that a close relationship with God requires clarity of mind, a focus on His will, and the ability to discern right from wrong. Alcohol, by impairing judgment and clouding the mind, makes it difficult to maintain this spiritual clarity. When someone is "swallowed up of wine," they are less able to connect with God, to hear His voice, and to follow His guidance. This spiritual disconnection is one of the most serious consequences of alcohol, as it leads to a loss of purpose, direction, and ultimately, salvation. The verse serves as a stark warning of the spiritual peril that comes with allowing alcohol to take control, urging individuals to stay vigilant and to avoid the path of excess that leads to spiritual ruin.

The image of leaders stumbling in judgment due to alcohol also speaks to the broader theme of the importance of integrity in leadership. The Bible often emphasizes the need for leaders to be wise, just, and righteous, as they are responsible for the well-being of those they lead. When alcohol impairs a leader's judgment, it compromises their ability to fulfill these responsibilities, leading to decisions that are not based on wisdom or justice. This lack of integrity can erode trust, undermine authority, and ultimately lead to the downfall of both the leader and those they lead. Isaiah 28:7's warning is a call to leaders to maintain their integrity by avoiding the pitfalls of alcohol, ensuring that their judgment remains clear and their decisions are guided by the principles of righteousness and justice.

Furthermore, the verse highlights the broader societal implications of alcohol abuse. When leaders—whether in government, religion, or community—are affected by alcohol, the entire society suffers. Laws may be unjust, decisions may be unfair, and the moral fabric of society may begin to unravel. The "stumbling" of leaders due to alcohol is not just a personal failing; it has the potential to lead to widespread harm, as the decisions they make affect the lives of many. This societal impact underscores the importance of maintaining sobriety and clear judgment, particularly for those in positions of authority. The dangers of alcohol, as highlighted in Isaiah 28:7, are thus not limited to the individual but have far-reaching consequences that can affect entire communities and nations.

In conclusion, Isaiah 28:7 provides a compelling and sobering warning about the dangers of alcohol, particularly its ability to cause individuals to stumble in judgment. The verse highlights how even those in positions of spiritual and moral authority can fall victim to the destructive power of alcohol, leading them to make poor decisions, lose their way, and ultimately fail in their responsibilities. The concept of "stumbling" is central to the verse, conveying the idea of losing one's footing both literally and metaphorically. Alcohol's ability to distort reality, impair judgment, and lead individuals "out of the way" is a powerful reminder of the dangers that come with its abuse. The verse's warning is not just about the immediate effects of alcohol but also about the long-term consequences, both personal and communal, that can result from a pattern of poor judgment and decision-making. The spiritual dangers of alcohol, as highlighted in the verse, are perhaps the most serious, as they lead to a disconnection from God and a loss of purpose and direction. The Bible's message is clear: the dangers of alcohol are real and far-reaching, and those who wish to lead with integrity, wisdom, and righteousness must avoid the path of excess that leads to stumbling in judgment. By heeding this warning, individuals and leaders alike can avoid the pitfalls of alcohol and maintain the clarity of mind and moral integrity needed to fulfill their responsibilities and live a life that is aligned with God's will.

Chapter 8 – The Sorrow

Proverbs 31:6-7, "Give strong drink unto him that is ready to perish, and wine unto those that be of heavy hearts. Let him drink, and forget his poverty, and remember his misery no more," speaks to the deep connection between sorrow and the consumption of alcohol, revealing how some people turn to drink in a desperate attempt to escape their pain. The verse acknowledges a reality that has been true across cultures and eras: when faced with overwhelming sorrow, grief, or hardship, people often seek solace in alcohol, hoping to numb their emotions and forget their troubles, even if just for a little while. This use of alcohol as a coping mechanism is highlighted in these verses as something that might seem to offer temporary relief, but in truth, it is a fleeting and dangerous escape. While the strong drink might momentarily dull the senses, the underlying sorrow, poverty, and misery are still there, lingering just beneath the surface, ready to resurface as soon as the effects of the alcohol wear off.

The concept of sorrow being masked by alcohol is one that resonates deeply with human experience. Many people, when confronted with the harsh realities of life—whether it be the loss of a loved one, financial ruin, loneliness, or any number of personal struggles—may feel that the weight of their sorrow is unbearable. In such times, alcohol can seem like an easy solution, a way to temporarily lift the heavy burden of grief or despair. The verses in Proverbs recognize this tendency, suggesting that those who are "ready to perish" or who are "of heavy hearts" might be given strong drink as a way to forget their suffering. However, this solution is presented with a sense of irony and caution. The idea is not that alcohol is a true remedy for sorrow, but rather that it offers a fleeting and ultimately ineffective respite from it.

The fleeting nature of alcohol's effect on sorrow is central to understanding the deeper message of these verses. When a person turns to alcohol to cope with sorrow, they are not addressing the root causes of their pain. Instead, they are merely covering it up, pushing it aside for a moment, but never truly healing from it. The temporary forgetfulness that alcohol provides can be seductive because it offers a break from the relentless pressure of sorrow. But as soon as the alcohol's effects fade, the sorrow returns, often with even greater intensity. This creates a cycle of dependence, where the individual feels compelled to drink again and again, each time hoping to escape their sorrow, but each time finding that the relief is only temporary and the pain remains. This cycle can lead to deeper emotional and physical harm, as the person becomes trapped in a pattern of drinking to forget, only to find that they can never truly escape their sorrow.

Moreover, the verses from Proverbs 31:6-7 highlight the particular danger of using alcohol to cope with poverty and misery. Poverty is often associated with a sense of hopelessness, a feeling that one's circumstances are beyond control and that there is no way out. In such a state, alcohol can become a false friend, offering a brief escape from the harsh realities of life. The idea of drinking to forget poverty and misery reflects a deep sense of despair, where a person feels that there is no other way to cope with their situation. However, while alcohol might provide temporary relief, it does nothing to change the person's circumstances. In fact, it can often make things worse. The money spent on alcohol could be used to improve one's situation, and the time spent drinking could be used to find solutions or seek help. Instead, the person becomes further entrenched in their poverty and misery, as the alcohol consumes not only their resources but also their hope and energy.

The sorrow that alcohol attempts to mask is also deeply connected to the emotional and psychological impact of grief and hardship. When a person is grieving or suffering, their emotions can feel overwhelming, as if they are drowning in their sorrow. Alcohol, in these moments, can seem like a life raft, something to cling to in order to stay afloat. However, this life raft is an illusion. Rather than helping the person navigate their grief, alcohol pulls them further into the depths of their sorrow, preventing them from finding real healing and peace. The verses from Proverbs suggest that while alcohol might allow a person to "forget" their misery for a time, it does not offer true comfort or resolution. The underlying sorrow remains, and until it is faced and dealt with, it will continue to haunt the individual, no matter how much they drink.

In addition, the use of alcohol to mask sorrow can lead to a host of other problems, both for the individual and for those around them. When a person relies on alcohol to cope with their emotions, they may become dependent on it, leading to addiction. This addiction can have devastating effects on all aspects of their life, including their relationships, work, and health. The person may become isolated, as their drinking alienates them from family and friends who may not understand their struggle or who are hurt by their behavior. Their work performance may suffer, leading to job loss and further financial difficulties. Their health may deteriorate, as excessive drinking takes a toll on the body, leading to conditions such as liver disease, heart problems, and mental health issues. The sorrow that alcohol was meant to alleviate is thus compounded by the additional suffering that comes with addiction.

Furthermore, the verses in Proverbs 31:6-7 also speak to the broader societal implications of using alcohol as a coping mechanism for sorrow. When individuals turn to alcohol to cope with their struggles, it can contribute to a culture of escapism, where people are encouraged to avoid their problems rather than confront them. This can lead to a society where issues such as poverty, inequality, and mental health are not adequately addressed because people are too focused on finding temporary relief rather than seeking long-term solutions. The normalization of using alcohol to mask sorrow can also perpetuate cycles of addiction and despair, as new generations learn to cope with their struggles in the same destructive ways as those before them. The verses from Proverbs serve as a cautionary tale, warning against the dangers of relying on alcohol to deal with life's challenges and encouraging people to seek healthier, more constructive ways of coping.

The message of Proverbs 31:6-7 is not just about the dangers of alcohol but also about the importance of finding true comfort and healing for our sorrows. While alcohol may offer a temporary escape, it does not provide the lasting peace and resolution that we need to truly heal from our pain. True comfort comes from addressing the root causes of our sorrow, whether that be through seeking help, connecting with others, or turning to our faith for guidance and strength. The Bible offers many other verses that speak to the power of God's love and the peace that comes from trusting in Him. Rather than turning to alcohol to forget our sorrows, we are encouraged to turn to God, who can provide the comfort and support we need to face our challenges and find true healing.

In addition, these verses remind us of the importance of supporting others who are struggling with sorrow. Rather than offering them alcohol as a way to forget their pain, we should offer them compassion, understanding, and help. We can play a crucial role in helping others find their way out of their misery by being there for them, listening to their struggles, and encouraging them to seek healthier ways of coping. This support can make a significant difference in their lives, helping them to avoid the pitfalls of alcohol and find a path to healing and recovery. The Bible calls us to love and care for one another, and part of that love is helping others avoid the dangers of alcohol and find true peace and comfort in their lives.

Moreover, the verses from Proverbs 31:6-7 also challenge us to reflect on our own coping mechanisms. When we face sorrow or hardship, how do we respond? Do we seek out temporary escapes, or do we confront our challenges head-on, seeking true resolution and healing? The Bible encourages us to be strong and courageous in the face of adversity, trusting that God is with us and that we can overcome our struggles with His help. By avoiding the temptation to mask our sorrow with alcohol or other temporary fixes, we can grow stronger, wiser, and more resilient, better equipped to handle whatever challenges life throws our way.

In conclusion, Proverbs 31:6-7 offers a powerful message about the dangers of using alcohol to mask sorrow. While it may offer a temporary escape, alcohol does not provide the lasting comfort and healing that we need to truly overcome our pain. Instead, it can lead to a cycle of dependence, further entrenching us in our sorrow and creating additional problems in our lives. The verses remind us of the importance of seeking true comfort and healing, whether through our faith, our relationships, or other constructive coping mechanisms. They also challenge us to support others who are struggling with sorrow, offering them compassion and help rather than temporary fixes. By heeding the warning of Proverbs 31:6-7, we can avoid the pitfalls of alcohol and find a path to true peace, healing, and fulfillment in our lives. The sorrow that alcohol may temporarily mask will always remain unless we address it directly and seek true resolution. Only then can we find the lasting comfort and strength that comes from facing our challenges head-on and trusting in the support and guidance of our faith, loved ones, and community.

Chapter 9 – The Strayed

1 Corinthians 5:11, "But now I have written unto you not to keep company, if any man that is called a brother be a fornicator, or covetous, or an idolater, or a railer, or a drunkard, or an extortioner; with such an one no not to eat," offers a powerful warning about the dangers of straying from the path of righteousness, particularly through the misuse of alcohol. The verse speaks to the serious consequences of allowing oneself to be led astray by behaviors that are not in alignment with the teachings of Christ, and it emphasizes the importance of maintaining a clear distinction between those who walk in righteousness and those who have chosen a path of sin. The specific mention of a "drunkard" in this list of sinful behaviors highlights the destructive nature of alcohol when it is abused, leading a person to stray far from the values and principles that are central to a life of faith.

To stray means to wander from the correct path, to deviate from the course that one is supposed to follow. In the context of 1 Corinthians 5:11, the path from which the drunkard has strayed is the path of righteousness, a path marked by self-control, wisdom, and a deep commitment to living according to God's will. When a person becomes a drunkard, they are not just indulging in a physical substance; they are allowing that substance to take control of their life, to cloud their judgment, and to lead them away from the values and beliefs that should guide their actions. The Bible warns that this kind of straying is dangerous not only for the individual but also for the community, which is why the apostle Paul instructs believers to avoid keeping company with those who have allowed themselves to be led astray in this way.

The idea of "no fellowship" with a drunkard is rooted in the understanding that fellowship, or close association, with someone who has strayed can be harmful to one's own spiritual health. The influence of a drunkard, who has allowed alcohol to dominate their life, can be corrosive, leading others to compromise their own values or to become desensitized to behaviors that are clearly against God's will. The Bible consistently teaches that believers are to be "in the world but not of the world," meaning that while we live in a world filled with temptation and sin, we are called to live differently, to maintain our commitment to God's standards, even when it is difficult. By avoiding close association with those who have strayed, particularly in the case of a drunkard, believers protect themselves from being drawn into similar behaviors and reinforce the importance of living a life that is in alignment with their faith.

Furthermore, the instruction to "not even eat" with such a person underscores the seriousness of the situation. Sharing a meal in biblical times was a sign of close fellowship and acceptance. To eat with someone was to express a level of intimacy and approval of their lifestyle. By advising believers to refrain from eating with a drunkard, Paul is emphasizing that the behavior of the drunkard is not to be condoned or accepted as normal. This is not about shunning or rejecting the person altogether but about making a clear statement that such behavior is not in line with the Christian way of life. It serves as a form of discipline, intended to prompt the individual to recognize their straying and to encourage them to return to the path of righteousness. The ultimate goal is not to alienate but to lead to repentance and restoration.

The notion of straying from righteousness through alcohol is further highlighted by the broader context of 1 Corinthians, where Paul addresses the importance of maintaining purity within the church community. The church is described as the body of Christ, and just as a physical body must be kept healthy by avoiding harmful substances, so too must the church be kept spiritually healthy by avoiding the influence of behaviors that are contrary to God's will. A drunkard, who has strayed from the path of righteousness, represents a threat to the spiritual health of the community, not because they are inherently evil, but because their behavior, if left unchecked, can spread and affect others. The Bible often uses the metaphor of yeast or leaven to describe how sin, if not addressed, can permeate and corrupt the whole community. The warning to avoid fellowship with a drunkard is, therefore, a protective measure, meant to preserve the integrity and holiness of the church.

Alcohol, when abused, has the power to lead people far from their intended path. It can dull the senses, impair judgment, and weaken the resolve to live according to God's standards. The verse in 1 Corinthians highlights how a person who becomes a drunkard has allowed alcohol to become a stumbling block, leading them away from the life they are called to live. This straying is not just a personal failing; it is a spiritual danger that affects not only the individual but also the entire community of believers. When someone is consumed by alcohol, they are no longer in control of their actions in a way that aligns with their faith. Instead, they are controlled by their desires, and this can lead to a downward spiral that is difficult to escape. The Bible's message is clear: the dangers of alcohol are real, and when it causes someone to stray from righteousness, it is something that must be addressed seriously.

The consequences of straying from righteousness through alcohol are not limited to the spiritual realm; they can also manifest in very real and tangible ways in a person's life. A drunkard may find themselves losing their job, their relationships, and their sense of purpose. The things that once mattered most can fall by the wayside as alcohol takes priority. The Bible warns that this kind of life leads to destruction, not just in the here and now but also in terms of one's eternal destiny. When a person allows alcohol to lead them away from the path of righteousness, they are not just jeopardizing their well-being in this life, but they are also putting their soul at risk. The warning in 1 Corinthians 5:11 serves as a call to wake up, to recognize the dangers of straying, and to take steps to return to the path that God has set before us.

The idea of straying also speaks to the concept of accountability within the Christian community. Believers are called to hold one another accountable, to encourage one another to stay on the right path, and to gently correct those who have strayed. The instruction to avoid fellowship with a drunkard is not about abandoning them but about encouraging them to see the error of their ways and to seek help. It is an act of tough love, meant to bring about repentance and restoration. The Bible teaches that we are our brother's keeper, and part of that responsibility involves helping others avoid the pitfalls of sin, including the dangers of alcohol. By refusing to condone or participate in the behavior of a drunkard, believers are sending a clear message that such behavior is not acceptable and that there is a better way to live.

In addition to the personal and communal consequences, the straying caused by alcohol also has broader societal implications. When individuals within a community, particularly those who are supposed to be role models, are led astray by alcohol, it can have a ripple effect that impacts others. Children who grow up in homes where alcohol abuse is prevalent may be more likely to struggle with substance abuse themselves. Communities where alcohol abuse is common may experience higher rates of crime, poverty, and social unrest. The Bible's warning to avoid fellowship with a drunkard is, therefore, not just about protecting the individual but about protecting the community as a whole. It is a call to create an environment where righteousness is upheld, and where the dangers of alcohol are recognized and addressed.

The verse also highlights the importance of making choices about who we associate with and how those associations affect our spiritual walk. While Christians are called to love and reach out to those who are struggling, they are also called to be wise about the influences they allow into their lives. Associating closely with someone who has strayed from righteousness can lead to compromise and can weaken one's own resolve to live according to God's standards. The Bible teaches that "bad company corrupts good character," and this principle is at play in the warning against keeping company with a drunkard. Believers are encouraged to surround themselves with others who are committed to walking in righteousness, who will support and encourage them in their faith, rather than pulling them away from it.

In conclusion, 1 Corinthians 5:11 provides a powerful and sobering message about the dangers of straying from the path of righteousness, particularly through the misuse of alcohol. The verse highlights how a drunkard, who has allowed alcohol to dominate their life, has strayed from the values and principles that are central to a life of faith. The instruction to avoid fellowship with such a person is not about rejection but about maintaining the integrity and holiness of the Christian community, protecting oneself and others from the corrosive influence of sin. The dangers of alcohol, as outlined in this verse, are far-reaching, affecting not only the individual but also the community and society as a whole. The Bible's message is clear: those who have strayed must be encouraged to return to the path of righteousness, and believers must be vigilant in protecting themselves from the dangers of alcohol. By heeding this warning, individuals and communities can avoid the pitfalls of straying and can live lives that are aligned with God's will, marked by self-control, wisdom, and a deep commitment to righteousness. The straying caused by alcohol is a serious danger, but with the support of a loving community and a commitment to living according to God's standards, it is possible to return to the right path and to live a life that honors God and brings true fulfillment.

Chapter 10 – The Sinful

Romans 13:13, "Let us walk honestly, as in the day; not in rioting and drunkenness, not in chambering and wantonness, not in strife and envying," serves as a powerful reminder of the connection between sinful behavior and the consumption of alcohol, specifically the dangers of drunkenness. This verse emphasizes the importance of living a life that is upright, transparent, and honest, akin to walking in the light of day where nothing is hidden. In contrast, it warns against behaviors associated with the darkness, including rioting, drunkenness, and other forms of immorality. The use of the word "drunkenness" in this context is particularly significant, as it highlights how excessive drinking can lead to a host of sinful behaviors, ultimately leading individuals away from the path of righteousness and deeper into the shadows of sin.

Drunkenness, as described in Romans 13:13, is more than just the act of consuming too much alcohol; it represents a state of being where one's judgment is impaired, self-control is lost, and the ability to make moral decisions is compromised. When a person becomes drunk, they open themselves up to a range of sinful behaviors that they might otherwise avoid. The verse warns against not only the act of drunkenness itself but also the actions that often accompany it, such as rioting, strife, and envy. These behaviors are the antithesis of the life that God calls us to live—lives marked by peace, self-control, and love for others. The Bible repeatedly stresses that drunkenness leads to a loss of self-control, which is a key component of a godly life. Without self-control, a person is more likely to engage in sinful activities, whether it's getting involved in fights (strife), giving in to jealousy (envy), or participating in reckless and immoral behavior (wantonness).

The connection between sinful behavior and drunkenness is not merely coincidental; it is deeply rooted in the nature of alcohol and its effects on the human mind and body. Alcohol has the power to dull the senses, lower inhibitions, and cloud judgment. When a person drinks excessively, they are more likely to say and do things that they would not consider in a sober state. This can lead to a range of sinful actions, from speaking harshly or engaging in arguments to making poor decisions that harm themselves and others. The verse from

Romans 13:13 is a clear warning that drunkenness is a doorway to sin, one that can lead to a cascade of negative consequences both in this life and in the eyes of God. By encouraging believers to avoid drunkenness, the Bible is urging them to maintain their integrity, to stay vigilant against temptation, and to live in a way that honors God and reflects His light.

Furthermore, the verse contrasts the behavior associated with drunkenness with the idea of walking "honestly, as in the day." This imagery of walking in the light of day suggests a life of transparency, where one's actions are visible, accountable, and aligned with moral and ethical standards. In contrast, drunkenness is linked with the darkness, where actions are hidden, uncontrolled, and often shameful. The Bible frequently uses the metaphor of light and darkness to distinguish between good and evil, righteousness and sin. By warning against drunkenness, Romans 13:13 is encouraging believers to live in the light, where their actions can stand up to scrutiny, where they can be proud of their choices, and where they are living in accordance with God's will. Drunkenness, on the other hand, is associated with the darkness, where people may try to hide their actions, where they lose sight of what is right, and where sin can easily take root and grow.

The sinful behaviors linked with drunkenness, as outlined in Romans 13:13, also have broader implications for one's relationships with others. Strife and envy, for example, are destructive forces that can tear apart friendships, families, and communities. When a person is drunk, they are more likely to engage in arguments, to act out of jealousy, and to create discord among those around them. The Bible teaches that believers are called to be peacemakers, to love their neighbors, and to build up the community of faith. Drunkenness undermines these values, leading instead to conflict, division, and harm. The verse serves as a warning that indulging in alcohol to the point of drunkenness not only harms the individual but also those around them, damaging relationships and sowing discord where there should be harmony and peace.

Moreover, the reference to "chambering and wantonness" in the verse speaks to the sexual immorality that is often associated with drunkenness. When a person is under the influence of alcohol, they are more likely to engage in behavior that they might otherwise avoid, including promiscuity, infidelity, and other forms of sexual sin. The Bible is clear in its teaching that sexual relations are to be reserved for the covenant of marriage, and that any sexual activity outside of this context is sinful. Drunkenness lowers the barriers that people might otherwise maintain, leading to decisions that are not only harmful to themselves but also to others. The consequences of such actions can be far-reaching, affecting not just the individuals involved but also their families, their communities, and their relationship with God. By warning against drunkenness, Romans 13:13 is also warning against the sexual sins that often accompany it, urging believers to maintain their purity and to honor God with their bodies as well as their actions.

The idea of walking "honestly, as in the day" also suggests a life of purpose and direction, in contrast to the aimlessness and lack of control associated with drunkenness. When a person is drunk, they are not in control of their actions; they are swayed by the effects of the alcohol, moving through life without a clear sense of direction or purpose. This can lead to a life that is marked by missed opportunities, poor decisions, and a failure to live up to one's potential. The Bible calls believers to live with intention, to make the most of the time and resources they have been given, and to pursue a life that is pleasing to God. Drunkenness, by contrast, leads to a life that is wasted, where time, talents, and opportunities are squandered in pursuit of temporary pleasure. Romans 13:13 is a call to rise above the distractions and temptations of this world, to live a life that is focused, purposeful, and aligned with the higher calling of following Christ.

In addition to the personal consequences, the sinful behavior linked with drunkenness can also have broader societal implications. Communities where drunkenness is prevalent often experience higher rates of crime, poverty, and social unrest. The Bible teaches that believers are to be a light in the world, to live in such a way that they bring positive change and reflect the love and justice of God. When drunkenness takes hold, it can lead to behaviors that undermine this mission, contributing to the very problems that believers are called to address. By warning against drunkenness, Romans 13:13 is also calling believers to be mindful of their role in society, to live in a way that promotes peace, justice, and the well-being of others, rather than contributing to the spread of sin and its destructive consequences.

The verse also speaks to the importance of self-control, a key aspect of living a life that is pleasing to God. Self-control is one of the fruits of the Spirit, a quality that allows believers to resist temptation, to make wise decisions, and to live in accordance with God's will. Drunkenness is the opposite of self-control; it represents a surrender to the desires of the flesh, a giving in to the temptation of excess and indulgence. The Bible is clear that believers are to exercise self-control in all areas of life, including the consumption of alcohol. By maintaining self-control, believers are able to stay on the path of righteousness, to avoid the pitfalls of sin, and to live in a way that honors God and reflects His character. Romans 13:13 serves as a reminder that self-control is not just a personal virtue but a spiritual necessity, one that is essential for avoiding the sinful behaviors that are linked with drunkenness.

In conclusion, Romans 13:13 provides a compelling and sobering message about the dangers of sinful behavior, particularly as it is linked with drunkenness. The verse warns against the loss of self-control, the impaired judgment, and the range of sinful actions that can result from excessive drinking. By contrasting the behaviors associated with drunkenness with the idea of walking "honestly, as in the day," the verse highlights the importance of living a life that is upright, transparent, and aligned with God's will. The sinful behaviors linked with drunkenness, including strife, envy, sexual immorality, and aimlessness, are destructive not only to the individual but also to relationships, communities, and society as a whole. The Bible's message is clear: believers are called to rise above these temptations, to live with self-control, and to walk in the light of God's truth. By avoiding the dangers of drunkenness, believers can maintain their integrity, stay focused on their higher calling, and live a life that is pleasing to God, free from the sinful behaviors that are linked with walking in darkness.

Chapter 11 – The Squandered Inheritance

Galatians 5:21, "Envyings, murders, drunkenness, revellings, and such like: of the which I tell you before, as I have also told you in time past, that they which do such things shall not inherit the kingdom of God," presents a solemn warning about the dangers of living a life marked by sin, particularly focusing on how such a lifestyle leads to a squandered inheritance. The verse lists various sinful behaviors, including drunkenness, and emphasizes that those who engage in these actions will not inherit the kingdom of God. This idea of a "squandered inheritance" is powerful, as it speaks to the eternal consequences of allowing oneself to be consumed by such behaviors, especially the destructive nature of drunkenness.

Inheritance, in the biblical sense, often refers to the blessings and promises that God has set aside for His people, both in this life and in the life to come. The kingdom of God represents the ultimate inheritance—a place of eternal peace, joy, and fellowship with God. It is the culmination of a life lived in faith, obedience, and righteousness. However, Galatians 5:21 makes it clear that those who choose to live in ways that are contrary to God's commands, such as indulging in drunkenness, risk forfeiting this precious inheritance. To squander something means to waste it thoughtlessly or recklessly, and in this context, it refers to the tragic loss of the eternal blessings that God offers to those who remain faithful to Him. When a person allows themselves to be drawn into a life of sin, particularly through the misuse of alcohol, they are not just jeopardizing their physical well-being or their relationships in this world; they are risking their eternal future.

The warning against drunkenness in Galatians 5:21 is particularly poignant because it highlights how alcohol can lead a person down a path of destruction, both spiritually and physically. Drunkenness is

more than just a temporary lapse in judgment; it is a state of being that
can open the door to a range of other sinful behaviors, such as those
listed in the verse—envy, murder, and revelry. These actions are not
isolated incidents; they are often the result of a lifestyle that has been
given over to excess, indulgence, and a disregard for the consequences.
The Bible frequently warns against the dangers of excess, urging
believers to practice self-control and to avoid anything that could lead
them away from the path of righteousness. Drunkenness, by its very
nature, erodes self-control, leading individuals to make decisions that
they would otherwise avoid. It dulls the senses, clouds judgment, and
makes it easier for other sins to take root in a person's life.

The concept of a "squandered inheritance" is further underscored
by the idea that those who engage in these sinful behaviors will not
inherit the kingdom of God. This inheritance is not something to be
taken lightly; it is the culmination of a life lived in faith and obedience
to God. To squander this inheritance is to throw away the most
precious gift that one could ever receive—eternal life with God. The
Bible is clear that salvation is a gift from God, but it also teaches that
how we live our lives matters. We are called to live in a way that reflects
our faith and our commitment to God's commands. When a person
chooses to live in drunkenness and other sinful behaviors, they are
essentially rejecting the inheritance that God has prepared for them.
This is a tragic waste, not just of the blessings that could be experienced
in this life, but of the eternal joy and peace that await those who remain
faithful.

The imagery of squandering an inheritance also brings to mind the
parable of the prodigal son, found in Luke 15:11-32. In this story, the
younger son demands his inheritance from his father, only to squander
it in a distant land through reckless living. Eventually, he finds himself
destitute and alone, having lost everything that his father had given
him. This parable mirrors the warning in Galatians 5:21, as it illustrates
how a life given over to excess and indulgence, such as drunkenness,

leads to ruin. The prodigal son's story ends with his return to the father and a restoration of his place in the family, symbolizing repentance and redemption. However, Galatians 5:21 reminds us that not everyone who squanders their inheritance through sinful living will find their way back. The stakes are incredibly high, as those who continue in such behaviors without repentance are warned that they will not inherit the kingdom of God.

The verse also serves as a call to self-reflection and examination of one's life choices. It challenges believers to consider whether their actions align with the life that God calls them to live. Are they living in a way that honors God and reflects His love, or are they allowing themselves to be led astray by the temptations of the world, such as drunkenness and other forms of excess? The Bible teaches that we are to be in the world but not of the world, meaning that while we live in a world filled with temptation, we are called to rise above it, to live according to God's standards rather than the world's. Drunkenness is one of the ways in which people can become entangled in the world's ways, losing sight of the higher calling that God has placed on their lives. The warning in Galatians 5:21 is a reminder that the choices we make have eternal consequences, and that we must be vigilant in guarding our hearts and minds against anything that could lead us away from God's path.

The idea of squandering an inheritance also speaks to the concept of stewardship, which is a recurring theme throughout the Bible. God has entrusted each of us with certain gifts, talents, and resources, and we are called to use them wisely and for His glory. When a person engages in drunkenness, they are not being good stewards of the life that God has given them. Instead, they are wasting the opportunities, time, and resources that could have been used to further God's kingdom and to bless others. The Bible teaches that we will all be held accountable for how we have used the gifts that God has given us, and those who have squandered these gifts through sinful living will face the consequences. Galatians 5:21 serves as a stark reminder that living a life of drunkenness and other sinful behaviors is a form of poor stewardship, one that leads not only to earthly consequences but also to the loss of the eternal inheritance that God has prepared for those who are faithful.

Furthermore, the verse highlights the importance of community and the influence that our choices have on others. In the early Christian church, as in today's church, the behavior of individual believers has a significant impact on the community as a whole. When a person chooses to live in drunkenness, they are not only endangering their own spiritual well-being but also potentially leading others astray. The Bible teaches that believers are to be examples to one another, encouraging and building each other up in faith. Drunkenness, however, can have the opposite effect, causing division, strife, and a weakening of the community's spiritual health. The warning in Galatians 5:21 is not just for the individual but for the community as a whole, as it calls believers to hold one another accountable and to encourage one another to live in a way that is worthy of the inheritance that God has promised.

The phrase "shall not inherit the kingdom of God" in Galatians 5:21 is particularly sobering because it emphasizes the finality of the consequences of living in sin. The kingdom of God represents the ultimate reward for those who have been born again. It is a place of eternal peace, joy, and fellowship with God, where all of the struggles and sorrows of this world are left behind. However, the verse makes it clear that those who choose to live in drunkenness and other sinful behaviors are choosing to forfeit this inheritance. This is not just a temporary loss but an eternal one, as those who do not inherit the kingdom of God will be separated from God's presence forever. The warning is clear: the choices we make in this life have eternal consequences, and those who choose to live in sin, including drunkenness, are choosing to squander the greatest inheritance that could ever be offered.

In conclusion, Galatians 5:21 offers a powerful and compelling warning about the dangers of living a life marked by sin, particularly focusing on the consequences of drunkenness. The verse highlights how such behaviors lead to a squandered inheritance, where the blessings and promises of God are lost due to a life of excess, indulgence, and disregard for God's commands. The idea of a squandered inheritance is a tragic one, as it represents the loss of the most precious gift that one could ever receive—eternal life in the kingdom of God. The Bible's message is clear: those who choose to live in drunkenness and other sinful behaviors are choosing to forfeit their inheritance, and the consequences are both serious and eternal. The verse serves as a call to self-reflection, urging believers to examine their lives and to make choices that align with God's will. It also speaks to the importance of stewardship, community, and accountability, reminding believers that their actions have a significant impact on both their own spiritual well-being and that of others. By heeding the warning in Galatians 5:21, believers can avoid the pitfalls of a life of sin and instead live in a way that honors God, reflects His love, and secures their place in His eternal kingdom. The squandered inheritance is a powerful reminder that the choices we make in this life matter, and that we must be vigilant in guarding against anything that could lead us away from the path of righteousness and toward a life of regret and loss.

Chapter 12 – The Selfish

Isaiah 28:1, "Woe to the crown of pride, to the drunkards of Ephraim, whose glorious beauty is a fading flower, which are on the head of the fat valleys of them that are overcome with wine!" paints a vivid picture of the destructive power of alcohol, highlighting how selfish indulgence in drunkenness leads to ruin. The verse begins with a pronouncement of "woe," a word often used in the Bible to signal deep sorrow, regret, or impending judgment. Here, the "crown of pride" refers to the leaders of Ephraim, a prominent tribe of Israel, who were once known for their strength and prosperity but have now become consumed by their own arrogance and excess. Their "glorious beauty" is likened to a fading flower, something that was once vibrant and full of life but is now wilting and dying because of their selfish indulgence in alcohol. The imagery of being "overcome with wine" underscores the idea that these leaders have allowed their lives to be dominated by their desire for alcohol, leading them away from the path of righteousness and toward a state of moral and spiritual decay.

The concept of selfishness is central to understanding the deeper message of Isaiah 28:1. To be selfish is to prioritize one's own desires and pleasures above the needs and well-being of others. In this context, the leaders of Ephraim have chosen to indulge in drunkenness, seeking their own pleasure and satisfaction without regard for the consequences. This selfish pursuit of pleasure has led them to neglect their responsibilities as leaders, abandoning their duty to care for and guide their people. Instead of using their power and influence to promote justice, righteousness, and the welfare of the community, they have turned inward, focusing solely on satisfying their own appetites. The Bible consistently warns against the dangers of selfishness, teaching that it leads to isolation, conflict, and ultimately, destruction. In the case of the drunkards of Ephraim, their selfish indulgence in alcohol has led to the fading of their once-glorious beauty and the erosion of their strength and influence.

The fading flower in Isaiah 28:1 is a powerful symbol of the transient nature of earthly pleasures and the inevitable decline that comes from a life of selfish indulgence. Just as a flower blooms brightly for a time but eventually withers and dies, so too does the beauty and strength of those who live a life dominated by selfish desires, particularly the desire for alcohol. The verse suggests that what was once a source of pride and glory for the leaders of Ephraim has now become a symbol of their downfall. Their focus on immediate gratification, on satisfying their own cravings for wine, has led them to neglect the things that truly matter—honor, integrity, and the well-being of their people. The Bible teaches that true beauty and strength come from living a life that is aligned with God's will, a life marked by self-control, humility, and a commitment to serving others. When these qualities are abandoned in favor of selfish indulgence, the result is a life that, like the fading flower, loses its vitality and purpose.

The phrase "overcome with wine" further emphasizes the idea of being overpowered or enslaved by one's desires. To be "overcome" suggests a loss of control, a state in which a person is no longer able to make rational decisions or exercise sound judgment. In the case of the drunkards of Ephraim, their selfish indulgence in alcohol has led them to a state where they are no longer in control of their actions or their lives. Instead, they are driven by their cravings, their minds clouded and their hearts hardened by their addiction to wine. The Bible often warns against allowing anything—whether it be alcohol, wealth, or power—to take control of one's life, teaching that true freedom and fulfillment come from living in accordance with God's commands and relying on His strength rather than our own. The leaders of Ephraim, by allowing themselves to be overcome with wine, have essentially surrendered their freedom and their ability to lead, becoming slaves to their own selfish desires.

The "crown of pride" mentioned in Isaiah 28:1 also speaks to the dangers of arrogance and self-centeredness. The leaders of Ephraim, in their pride, believed that they were invincible, that their strength and prosperity would last forever. They saw their wealth and power as a crown, a symbol of their superiority and success. However, their pride blinded them to the reality of their situation—that their selfish indulgence in alcohol was leading them to ruin. The Bible teaches that pride goes before a fall, and in the case of Ephraim, their pride has led them to a place where their once-glorious beauty is fading, their strength is diminishing, and their influence is waning. The "crown of pride" has become a symbol of their downfall, a reminder that when we place our trust in our own abilities and seek to satisfy our own desires above all else, we set ourselves on a path that leads to destruction.

The verse also highlights the broader impact of the leaders' selfish indulgence on the community as a whole. The leaders of Ephraim were not just responsible for their own lives; they were entrusted with the care and guidance of their people. Their role was to lead by example, to promote justice, righteousness, and the welfare of the community. However, their selfish pursuit of pleasure through alcohol led them to neglect these responsibilities, leaving the people of Ephraim without the leadership and support they needed. The Bible teaches that leadership is a sacred trust, one that requires humility, selflessness, and a commitment to the greater good. When leaders fail to uphold these values, the consequences are felt not just by themselves but by the entire community. The selfishness of the drunkards of Ephraim led to the weakening of their people, the erosion of their moral and spiritual foundations, and the eventual decline of their society.

Moreover, the verse serves as a cautionary tale for all who are tempted to prioritize their own desires above their responsibilities to others. The Bible consistently teaches that we are called to love our neighbors as ourselves, to seek the well-being of others, and to live lives that are marked by selflessness and service. When we allow selfish desires, such as the craving for alcohol, to take precedence in our lives, we not only harm ourselves but also those around us. The drunkards of Ephraim, in their selfish pursuit of pleasure, became a stumbling block to their people, leading them away from the path of righteousness and toward a state of moral and spiritual decay. The warning in Isaiah 28:1 is clear: when we allow ourselves to be consumed by selfish desires, we risk losing everything that truly matters—our integrity, our relationships, and our standing before God.

The imagery of the "fat valleys" in Isaiah 28:1 also underscores the idea of abundance and prosperity that has been squandered through selfish indulgence. The valleys of Ephraim were once fertile and fruitful, a source of wealth and sustenance for the people. However, the leaders, in their selfish pursuit of pleasure through alcohol, failed to steward this abundance wisely. Instead of using their resources to benefit the community and promote the common good, they squandered them on their own selfish desires. The Bible teaches that we are called to be good stewards of the resources that God has entrusted to us, using them to serve others and advance His kingdom. When we fail to do so, when we use our resources to satisfy our own cravings rather than to fulfill our responsibilities, we set ourselves on a path that leads to ruin. The "fat valleys" of Ephraim, once a symbol of prosperity, have become a symbol of wasted potential and lost opportunities, a reminder of the consequences of selfish indulgence.

In conclusion, Isaiah 28:1 offers a powerful and sobering message about the dangers of selfish indulgence, particularly through the misuse of alcohol. The verse highlights how the leaders of Ephraim, once known for their strength and prosperity, allowed themselves to be overcome with wine, leading them away from the path of righteousness and toward a state of moral and spiritual decay. The "crown of pride" that they once wore with arrogance and self-assurance has become a symbol of their downfall, as their selfish pursuit of pleasure led to the fading of their once-glorious beauty and the erosion of their strength and influence. The Bible's message is clear: when we prioritize our own desires above our responsibilities to others, when we allow selfishness to guide our actions, we set ourselves on a path that leads to ruin. The story of the drunkards of Ephraim serves as a cautionary tale for all who are tempted to indulge in selfish desires, particularly the desire for alcohol, reminding us that true beauty and strength come from living a life that is aligned with God's will, marked by self-control, humility, and a commitment to serving others. By heeding the warning in Isaiah 28:1, we can avoid the pitfalls of selfish indulgence and instead live lives that are characterized by selflessness, service, and a steadfast commitment to righteousness. The consequences of selfish indulgence are clear: it leads to the fading of what is truly beautiful and the loss of what is truly valuable, both in this life and in the life to come.

Chapter 13 – The Shattered

Deuteronomy 21:20, "And they shall say unto the elders of his city, This our son is stubborn and rebellious, he will not obey our voice; he is a glutton, and a drunkard," provides a powerful and sobering illustration of how lives can be utterly shattered by the grip of alcohol. This verse captures the heartache and despair of parents who have watched their child descend into a life of stubborn rebellion, gluttony, and drunkenness, ultimately leading to a complete breakdown in the relationship between parent and child, and the shattering of the child's future. The term "shattered" perfectly encapsulates the devastating consequences of a life dominated by alcohol, where dreams, relationships, and potential are broken beyond repair, leaving nothing but fragments of what could have been.

The word "shattered" brings to mind the image of something that has been broken into countless pieces, something that was once whole and functional but has now been destroyed. In the context of this verse, it reflects the tragic outcome of a life consumed by alcohol. A person who becomes a drunkard, according to this verse, is not just someone who occasionally drinks too much; they are someone whose life has become dominated and controlled by alcohol to the point where they have lost all sense of responsibility, obedience, and respect for themselves and others. The parents' plea in this verse highlights their deep sorrow and frustration as they witness their child's life fall apart. Their son, once full of potential and promise, has become unrecognizable—a stubborn, rebellious drunkard whose life is in ruins.

The verse also speaks to the impact of such behavior on the family and community. The parents are not just dealing with their son's rebellion and drunkenness in private; they are compelled to bring the matter before the elders of the city, making it a public issue. This reflects the broader societal implications of a life shattered by alcohol. When someone succumbs to the grip of alcohol, the consequences are not limited to the individual. Families suffer, relationships are strained or broken, and the community is impacted. The verse suggests that the son's behavior has become so destructive that it can no longer be ignored or handled privately—it must be addressed by the community at large. This public acknowledgment of the problem underscores the seriousness of the situation and the extent to which alcohol can destroy lives.

The stubbornness and rebellion mentioned in the verse also highlight the way that alcohol can harden a person's heart and mind, making them resistant to guidance, correction, and love. When a person becomes a drunkard, they are not just physically intoxicated; they are also often spiritually and emotionally intoxicated, losing their ability to listen to reason, to accept help, and to change their ways. The Bible frequently warns against hard-heartedness, teaching that it leads to a path of destruction. In this case, the son's stubbornness and rebellion are directly linked to his gluttony and drunkenness, suggesting that his addiction to alcohol has not only destroyed his physical health but also his ability to make sound decisions, to respect his parents, and to live a life of integrity. This kind of hard-heartedness is one of the most tragic outcomes of a life shattered by alcohol, as it closes off the possibility of redemption and healing.

The verse also emphasizes the role of the community in addressing the problem of drunkenness. In ancient Israel, the elders of the city played a crucial role in maintaining order and justice, and they were responsible for addressing serious issues within the community. The fact that the parents bring their son to the elders indicates that his behavior has reached a point where it is not just a personal or family issue but a community concern. This reflects the broader truth that when lives are shattered by alcohol, the effects are felt far beyond the individual and their immediate family. Communities must grapple with the consequences of alcoholism, whether it's through increased crime, strained social services, or the emotional toll on families and neighbors. The Bible's message here is clear: the problem of alcohol cannot be ignored or swept under the rug. It must be confronted openly and addressed with the seriousness it deserves, both for the sake of the individual and the community as a whole.

Moreover, the verse brings attention to the wasted potential of the son's life. The parents' despair is not just about the immediate consequences of their son's behavior; it's also about the loss of what could have been. Their son had the potential to live a full, productive life, to contribute to his community, to build a family, and to walk in the ways of righteousness. But all of that potential has been shattered by his decision to give in to gluttony and drunkenness. The Bible consistently teaches that each person is created with a purpose and a calling, and that our lives are meant to reflect the goodness and glory of God. When someone chooses a path of drunkenness, they are not just harming themselves; they are rejecting the potential that God has placed within them, choosing instead to live a life that leads to destruction. The son's life, as described in this verse, is a tragic example of potential that has been wasted and a future that has been lost.

The verse also speaks to the finality of the consequences that come with a life of drunkenness. The fact that the parents feel compelled to bring their son to the elders suggests that they have exhausted all other options; they have tried to reach him, to correct him, to bring him back to the right path, but to no avail. Now, they are left with no choice but to hand him over to the community for judgment. This sense of finality is one of the most devastating aspects of a life shattered by alcohol. When a person's life becomes dominated by alcohol, the consequences can be irreversible. Relationships can be damaged beyond repair, health can be destroyed, and opportunities can be lost forever. The Bible's warning here is stark: the choices we make, particularly when it comes to alcohol, have serious and lasting consequences. A life of drunkenness can lead to a point of no return, where the damage is so great that it cannot be undone.

The idea of a shattered life also extends to the spiritual consequences of drunkenness. The Bible teaches that our bodies are temples of the Holy Spirit and that we are called to honor God with our bodies. When a person chooses a life of gluttony and drunkenness, they are not only harming their physical body but also their spiritual well-being. Drunkenness can lead to a separation from God, as the person becomes more focused on satisfying their own desires than on living a life that is pleasing to God. The stubbornness and rebellion described in the verse are not just directed at the parents but also at God Himself. The son's refusal to obey and his decision to live a life of excess are a rejection of the life that God has called him to live. The spiritual consequences of such a life are severe, leading to a broken relationship with God and the loss of the peace, joy, and purpose that come from walking in His ways.

The verse also serves as a warning to others who might be tempted to follow the same path. The public nature of the judgment in this verse is meant to serve as a deterrent, to show others the consequences of a life of stubbornness, rebellion, and drunkenness. The Bible frequently uses examples of those who have fallen into sin as warnings to others, urging them to choose a different path. In this case, the shattered life of the son is a powerful reminder of what can happen when we allow ourselves to be overcome by our desires. The Bible's message is clear: drunkenness leads to ruin, not just for the individual but for their family, their community, and their relationship with God. By heeding this warning, others can avoid the same fate and choose a life that is marked by self-control, obedience, and a commitment to living in accordance with God's will.

In conclusion, Deuteronomy 21:20 offers a powerful and sobering message about the dangers of a life dominated by drunkenness. The verse vividly depicts how such a life can lead to shattered relationships, wasted potential, and irreversible consequences. The stubbornness and rebellion that come with a life of gluttony and drunkenness are not just personal failings; they are actions that have profound effects on the individual, their family, and their community. The public nature of the judgment in this verse underscores the seriousness of the issue and the need for the community to address it openly and decisively. The Bible's message is clear: a life of drunkenness leads to ruin, both physically and spiritually. The consequences are severe and lasting, often leading to a point of no return. By choosing a life of self-control, obedience, and humility, we can avoid the pitfalls of drunkenness and live lives that reflect the goodness and glory of God. The shattered life of the son in this verse serves as a powerful warning to others, reminding us of the importance of making wise choices and living in accordance with God's will. The consequences of a life of drunkenness are clear: it leads to the destruction of everything that truly matters—our relationships, our potential, our community, and our relationship with God. By heeding this warning, we can choose a different path, one that leads to life, peace, and fulfillment in God's kingdom.

Chapter 14 – The Stagnation

1 Peter 4:3, "For the time past of our life may suffice us to have wrought the will of the Gentiles, when we walked in lasciviousness, lusts, excess of wine, revellings, banquetings, and abominable idolatries," offers a poignant reflection on the dangers of living a life consumed by worldly desires, particularly the excessive consumption of alcohol. This verse, penned by the Apostle Peter, speaks directly to the believers, reminding them of their past lives when they were ensnared by the very things that are now to be left behind. The term "stagnation" perfectly captures the spiritual state of those who continue to indulge in such behaviors, especially in the excess of wine. Stagnation, in this context, refers to the lack of progress, growth, or movement in one's spiritual journey, caused by the continuous indulgence in behaviors that are contrary to the will of God. Just as stagnant water becomes stale and lifeless, so too does a life that is mired in excessive drinking and other sinful pleasures. Such a life is marked by a failure to grow, to change, and to move forward in one's relationship with God.

The verse begins by acknowledging the past, a time when the believers once walked in the ways of the Gentiles, meaning they lived according to the desires of their flesh rather than the will of God. This past life, characterized by lasciviousness, lusts, excess of wine, revelings, banquetings, and idolatries, is depicted as a period of spiritual darkness and futility. The excessive indulgence in wine, in particular, is singled out as a behavior that leads to spiritual stagnation. When a person gives themselves over to excessive drinking, they are not just engaging in a physical act; they are allowing their spiritual growth to come to a halt. The excess of wine dulls the senses, clouds judgment, and makes it difficult for a person to connect with God or to pursue the things that truly matter in life. It creates a barrier between the individual and the spiritual progress they are called to make.

Stagnation in spiritual growth is one of the most dangerous consequences of living a life marked by excess wine. The Bible consistently teaches that believers are to grow in their faith, to become more like Christ, and to continually strive for holiness and righteousness. This growth requires intentional effort, discipline, and a commitment to turning away from the things that hinder our progress. However, when a person is caught up in the excess of wine and other worldly pleasures, they become spiritually stagnant. Their focus shifts away from God and His purposes, and instead, they become consumed by the temporary and fleeting pleasures of this world. The verse from 1 Peter 4:3 reminds believers that the time for such behaviors has passed and that continuing to live in this way is a refusal to move forward in their spiritual journey.

The imagery of walking in "lasciviousness, lusts, excess of wine, revelings, banquetings, and abominable idolatries" paints a picture of a life that is bound by the desires of the flesh. These behaviors are not just random acts of sin; they represent a way of life that is deeply entrenched in self-indulgence and rebellion against God. The excess of wine, in particular, is associated with a loss of self-control and a surrender to the baser instincts of human nature. When a person is consumed by alcohol, they lose their ability to think clearly, to make wise decisions, and to live in a way that honors God. This loss of control leads to stagnation, as the person becomes trapped in a cycle of indulgence and sin, unable to break free and move forward in their spiritual life. The verse serves as a stark warning that living in this way is not only unproductive but also destructive to one's spiritual health.

Moreover, the reference to "the will of the Gentiles" in the verse underscores the contrast between a life lived according to the desires of the flesh and a life lived according to the will of God. The Gentiles, in this context, represent those who do not know God and who live according to their own desires rather than seeking to do what is right in God's eyes. The excess of wine and other sinful behaviors are seen as characteristic of this way of life, a life that is devoid of spiritual growth and purpose. For the believer, however, there is a higher calling—a call to live in the light, to pursue holiness, and to grow in their relationship with God. Stagnation occurs when a person continues to live as they did before knowing Christ, refusing to leave behind the old ways and embrace the new life that God offers. The verse challenges believers to recognize that their past life, marked by excess and indulgence, is no longer acceptable and that they must move forward in their spiritual journey.

The idea of spiritual stagnation is also closely tied to the concept of repentance and transformation. The Bible teaches that when a person comes to Christ, they are a new creation—the old has passed away, and the new has come. This transformation is not just a one-time event but an ongoing process of growth and change. However, when a person continues to indulge in behaviors like the excess of wine, they are resisting this transformation, clinging to the old ways rather than embracing the new life that God has for them. This resistance leads to stagnation, as the person is unable to experience the fullness of life that God intends for them. The verse from 1 Peter 4:3 is a call to repentance, urging believers to turn away from the excess of wine and other sinful behaviors and to pursue a life of spiritual growth and transformation.

The mention of "revelings" and "banquetings" in the verse further emphasizes the idea of indulgence and excess. These terms refer to wild parties and feasts where the focus is on satisfying the desires of the flesh rather than honoring God. Such activities are often associated with excessive drinking, gluttony, and immoral behavior. The Bible teaches that believers are to live in moderation, exercising self-control and avoiding anything that would lead them away from God. However, when a person is caught up in revelings and banquetings, they are living for the moment, seeking pleasure and satisfaction in things that are ultimately empty and unfulfilling. This focus on the immediate, the physical, and the temporal leads to stagnation, as the person is unable to see beyond their current circumstances and to pursue the deeper, more meaningful things of life.

The verse also highlights the connection between excess wine and "abominable idolatries." In the Bible, idolatry refers to the worship of false gods or the placing of anything above God in one's life. When a person indulges in the excess of wine, they are essentially placing their desire for alcohol above their desire for God. This becomes a form of idolatry, as the person is worshipping the created thing (wine) rather than the Creator. The Bible is clear that idolatry is a serious sin, as it leads a person away from God and into spiritual darkness. The verse from 1 Peter 4:3 warns that this kind of idolatry leads to stagnation, as the person is unable to grow in their relationship with God when they are focused on satisfying their own desires. The challenge for believers is to identify and remove any idols in their lives, including the excess of wine, so that they can fully commit to their spiritual growth and walk with God.

Furthermore, the verse serves as a reminder that the time for such behaviors has passed. The phrase "For the time past of our life may suffice us" suggests that there has already been enough time spent in the pursuit of these worldly desires. The call now is to leave these things behind and to move forward in a new direction. This call to move forward is essential to overcoming stagnation, as it requires a conscious decision to change, to grow, and to pursue the things of God. The verse challenges believers to evaluate their lives and to ask themselves whether they are still holding on to the excesses of the past or whether they are truly committed to growing in their faith. It is a call to action, to step out of the darkness of the past and into the light of a new life in Christ.

In conclusion, 1 Peter 4:3 provides a powerful and compelling message about the dangers of spiritual stagnation caused by the excess of wine and other sinful behaviors. The verse reminds believers of the past life they once lived, a life characterized by indulgence, excess, and a lack of spiritual growth. It warns that continuing to live in this way leads to stagnation, a state in which spiritual progress comes to a halt and the person is unable to grow in their relationship with God. The verse challenges believers to recognize that the time for such behaviors has passed and that they must now move forward in their spiritual journey. It emphasizes the importance of leaving behind the old ways and embracing the new life that God has for them—a life marked by self-control, holiness, and a commitment to spiritual growth. By heeding this warning, believers can avoid the pitfalls of stagnation and instead live lives that are vibrant, purposeful, and fully aligned with the will of God. The dangers of excess wine are clear: it leads to a life that is stagnant, unproductive, and disconnected from God. The call is to rise above these temptations, to leave behind the excesses of the past, and to pursue a life of spiritual growth, transformation, and deepening relationship with God.

Chapter 15 – The Shortsighted

Luke 21:34, "And take heed to yourselves, lest at any time your hearts be overcharged with surfeiting, and drunkenness, and cares of this life, and so that day come upon you unawares," delivers a poignant and urgent warning about the dangers of shortsighted living, particularly when it is marred by indulgence in alcohol. Jesus' words here serve as a stark reminder that living in the present moment without regard for the future can lead to spiritual disaster. The concept of being "shortsighted" refers to the inability to see beyond the immediate, to recognize the long-term consequences of one's actions, and to prepare adequately for what is to come. In the context of this scripture, shortsightedness manifests as an excessive focus on worldly pleasures—such as overindulgence in food and drink (surfeiting and drunkenness)—and the distractions of daily life, which can cause a person to miss the most important event of all: the coming of the Lord.

The verse begins with a command to "take heed to yourselves," urging believers to be vigilant and self-aware. This is not merely a suggestion but a critical directive meant to protect one's spiritual well-being. The warning is clear: if we allow ourselves to be consumed by the temporary pleasures and concerns of this life, we risk being unprepared for Christ's return. The imagery of being "overcharged" conveys the idea of being weighed down or burdened, as if one's heart and mind are so clogged with earthly matters that they can no longer focus on what truly matters. Drunkenness, in particular, is highlighted as a significant danger, as it represents a state of mind where clarity and discernment are lost. When someone is drunk, they are not thinking about the future or about spiritual matters; they are absorbed in the here and now, seeking immediate gratification without concern for the consequences. This shortsightedness can be spiritually fatal, as it leads to a life that is unprepared for the Lord's coming.

Drunkenness, as described in this verse, is not just a physical state but a metaphor for a life that is out of control, unfocused, and disconnected from spiritual reality. When a person indulges in alcohol to the point of drunkenness, they are effectively blinding themselves to the truths that should guide their lives. Their priorities become skewed, with immediate pleasures taking precedence over eternal values. The Bible consistently teaches that we are to live with eternity in mind, making choices that reflect our faith and our anticipation of Christ's return. However, when a person is caught up in drunkenness and the cares of this life, they lose sight of this eternal perspective. They become shortsighted, unable to see beyond their current circumstances and the temporary satisfaction that alcohol provides. This lack of foresight is dangerous because it leads to a life that is unprepared for the return of Christ, a day that will come unexpectedly and without warning.

The verse also emphasizes the idea of being "overcharged" with the "cares of this life." This phrase speaks to the many distractions and concerns that can occupy our minds and hearts, pulling us away from our spiritual focus. In today's world, it is easy to become overwhelmed by the demands of daily life—work, family, finances, and social obligations—all of which can consume our time and energy. While these things are not inherently bad, the danger lies in allowing them to dominate our lives to the point where we neglect our spiritual responsibilities. When we are "overcharged" with these cares, we become shortsighted, focusing only on the immediate needs and concerns rather than on the bigger picture of our spiritual journey. Drunkenness exacerbates this problem by further clouding our judgment and dulling our awareness of spiritual realities. It creates a false sense of security, where the person feels momentarily at ease but is actually drifting further from the readiness that Christ calls us to maintain.

Jesus' warning in Luke 21:34 is particularly urgent because it speaks to the suddenness of His return. The phrase "and so that day come upon you unawares" underscores the idea that Christ's return will be unexpected, like a thief in the night. Those who are living in a state of shortsightedness, consumed by drunkenness and the cares of this life, will be caught off guard. They will not have the time or presence of mind to prepare themselves, and they will face the consequences of their unpreparedness. The Bible repeatedly stresses the importance of being watchful, staying alert, and living each day as if Christ could return at any moment. However, those who are shortsighted, who are focused on the pleasures and distractions of this world, are not living in a state of readiness. They are living for the moment, unaware of the spiritual dangers that lurk just beyond their sight. This shortsighted approach to life is perilous because it ignores the reality of Christ's return and the judgment that will follow.

Furthermore, the verse highlights the broader implications of a life marked by drunkenness and shortsightedness. When a person is consumed by alcohol and the cares of this life, they are not only jeopardizing their own spiritual well-being but also their ability to positively influence others. The Bible calls believers to be salt and light in the world, to live in a way that reflects God's love and truth to those around them. However, when someone is caught up in drunkenness, their witness is compromised. Their actions and attitudes do not point others to Christ but instead reflect the very worldliness that they are supposed to stand against. This failure to live out the gospel not only affects the individual but also weakens the testimony of the broader Christian community. The shortsightedness that comes with drunkenness leads to a life that is ineffective in fulfilling the Great Commission, as the person is too preoccupied with their own desires and concerns to focus on the mission that God has given them.

The idea of shortsightedness also ties into the concept of spiritual maturity. The Bible teaches that as believers, we are to grow in our faith, becoming more like Christ and deepening our understanding of His will. This growth requires discipline, self-control, and a focus on the things that matter most—our relationship with God, our service to others, and our preparation for Christ's return. However, when a person is shortsighted, they are stunted in their spiritual growth. They are like children, focused on immediate gratification rather than long-term goals. Drunkenness, with its emphasis on the here and now, prevents a person from developing the maturity and wisdom that come with a life lived in close communion with God. This spiritual immaturity is dangerous because it leaves the person vulnerable to temptation and unprepared for the challenges and responsibilities of the Christian life. The verse from Luke 21:34 is a call to move beyond this shortsightedness, to cultivate a mature faith that looks beyond the immediate and prepares for the eternal.

Moreover, the verse serves as a reminder that life is fleeting, and the time we have to prepare for Christ's return is limited. The Bible teaches that our lives are like a vapor, here today and gone tomorrow. In light of this, it is crucial that we make the most of the time we have, focusing on the things that have eternal significance rather than being consumed by temporary pleasures. Drunkenness, and the shortsightedness that accompanies it, squanders this precious time, leading to a life that is unproductive and unprepared. Jesus' warning in Luke 21:34 is a wake-up call to those who are living for the moment, urging them to shift their focus to the things that truly matter. It is a call to live with the end in mind, to recognize that the choices we make today have eternal consequences, and to ensure that we are ready for Christ's return.

The concept of shortsightedness in this verse also speaks to the broader issue of spiritual awareness. The Bible calls believers to be spiritually alert, to discern the times, and to live in a way that reflects their understanding of God's plan. However, when a person is caught up in drunkenness and the cares of this life, their spiritual senses are dulled. They become unaware of the spiritual realities that surround them, missing the signs of the times and failing to recognize the urgency of the hour. This lack of awareness is dangerous because it leads to complacency, a false sense of security that everything is fine when in reality, the day of the Lord is drawing near. The verse from Luke 21:34 challenges believers to stay spiritually awake, to avoid the distractions and temptations that lead to shortsightedness, and to live in a state of readiness for Christ's return.

In conclusion, Luke 21:34 offers a powerful and urgent warning about the dangers of shortsighted living, particularly when it is marked by drunkenness and an excessive focus on the cares of this life. The verse calls believers to "take heed" to themselves, to be vigilant and self-aware, and to avoid the traps that can lead to spiritual stagnation and unpreparedness. Drunkenness, in particular, is highlighted as a significant danger, as it clouds judgment, dulls spiritual awareness, and leads to a life that is focused on immediate gratification rather than eternal realities. The shortsightedness that comes with such a lifestyle is perilous because it leads to a life that is unprepared for the most important event of all: the return of Christ. The Bible calls believers to live with eternity in mind, to make choices that reflect their faith and their anticipation of Christ's coming. By heeding the warning in Luke 21:34, believers can avoid the pitfalls of shortsightedness, cultivate spiritual maturity, and live lives that are ready for the Lord's return. The dangers of shortsighted living are clear: it leads to a life that is unproductive, unprepared, and disconnected from the spiritual realities that truly matter. The call is to rise above these distractions, to live with purpose and focus, and to ensure that we are ready for the day when Christ returns.

Chapter 16 – The Severed

Luke 21:34, "And take heed to yourselves, lest at any time your hearts be overcharged with surfeiting, and drunkenness, and cares of this life, and so that day come upon you unawares," delivers a poignant and urgent warning about the dangers of shortsighted living, particularly when it is marred by indulgence in alcohol. Jesus' words here serve as a stark reminder that living in the present moment without regard for the future can lead to spiritual disaster. The concept of being "shortsighted" refers to the inability to see beyond the immediate, to recognize the long-term consequences of one's actions, and to prepare adequately for what is to come. In the context of this scripture, shortsightedness manifests as an excessive focus on worldly pleasures—such as overindulgence in food and drink (surfeiting and drunkenness)—and the distractions of daily life, which can cause a person to miss the most important event of all: the coming of the Lord.

The verse begins with a command to "take heed to yourselves," urging believers to be vigilant and self-aware. This is not merely a suggestion but a critical directive meant to protect one's spiritual well-being. The warning is clear: if we allow ourselves to be consumed by the temporary pleasures and concerns of this life, we risk being unprepared for Christ's return. The imagery of being "overcharged" conveys the idea of being weighed down or burdened, as if one's heart and mind are so clogged with earthly matters that they can no longer focus on what truly matters. Drunkenness, in particular, is highlighted as a significant danger, as it represents a state of mind where clarity and discernment are lost. When someone is drunk, they are not thinking about the future or about spiritual matters; they are absorbed in the here and now, seeking immediate gratification without concern for the consequences. This shortsightedness can be spiritually fatal, as it leads to a life that is unprepared for the Lord's coming.

Drunkenness, as described in this verse, is not just a physical state but a metaphor for a life that is out of control, unfocused, and disconnected from spiritual reality. When a person indulges in alcohol to the point of drunkenness, they are effectively blinding themselves to the truths that should guide their lives. Their priorities become skewed, with immediate pleasures taking precedence over eternal values. The

Bible consistently teaches that we are to live with eternity in mind, making choices that reflect our faith and our anticipation of Christ's return. However, when a person is caught up in drunkenness and the cares of this life, they lose sight of this eternal perspective. They become shortsighted, unable to see beyond their current circumstances and the temporary satisfaction that alcohol provides. This lack of foresight is dangerous because it leads to a life that is unprepared for the return of Christ, a day that will come unexpectedly and without warning.

The verse also emphasizes the idea of being "overcharged" with the "cares of this life." This phrase speaks to the many distractions and concerns that can occupy our minds and hearts, pulling us away from our spiritual focus. In today's world, it is easy to become overwhelmed by the demands of daily life—work, family, finances, and social obligations—all of which can consume our time and energy. While these things are not inherently bad, the danger lies in allowing them to dominate our lives to the point where we neglect our spiritual responsibilities. When we are "overcharged" with these cares, we become shortsighted, focusing only on the immediate needs and concerns rather than on the bigger picture of our spiritual journey. Drunkenness exacerbates this problem by further clouding our judgment and dulling our awareness of spiritual realities. It creates a false sense of security, where the person feels momentarily at ease but is actually drifting further from the readiness that Christ calls us to maintain.

Jesus' warning in Luke 21:34 is particularly urgent because it speaks to the suddenness of His return. The phrase "and so that day come upon you unawares" underscores the idea that Christ's return will be unexpected, like a thief in the night. Those who are living in a state of shortsightedness, consumed by drunkenness and the cares of this life, will be caught off guard. They will not have the time or presence of mind to prepare themselves, and they will face the consequences of their unpreparedness. The Bible repeatedly stresses the importance of being watchful, staying alert, and living each day as if Christ could return at any moment. However, those who are shortsighted, who are focused on the pleasures and distractions of this world, are not living in a state of readiness. They are living for the moment, unaware of the spiritual dangers that lurk just beyond their sight. This shortsighted approach to life is perilous because it ignores the reality of Christ's return and the judgment that will follow.

Furthermore, the verse highlights the broader implications of a life marked by drunkenness and shortsightedness. When a person is consumed by alcohol and the cares of this life, they are not only jeopardizing their own spiritual well-being but also their ability to positively influence others. The Bible calls believers to be salt and light in the world, to live in a way that reflects God's love and truth to those around them. However, when someone is caught up in drunkenness, their witness is compromised. Their actions and attitudes do not point others to Christ but instead reflect the very worldliness that they are supposed to stand against. This failure to live out the gospel not only affects the individual but also weakens the testimony of the broader Christian community. The shortsightedness that comes with drunkenness leads to a life that is ineffective in fulfilling the Great Commission, as the person is too preoccupied with their own desires and concerns to focus on the mission that God has given them.

The idea of shortsightedness also ties into the concept of spiritual maturity. The Bible teaches that as believers, we are to grow in our faith, becoming more like Christ and deepening our understanding of His will. This growth requires discipline, self-control, and a focus on the things that matter most—our relationship with God, our service to others, and our preparation for Christ's return. However, when a person is shortsighted, they are stunted in their spiritual growth. They are like children, focused on immediate gratification rather than long-term goals. Drunkenness, with its emphasis on the here and now, prevents a person from developing the maturity and wisdom that come with a life lived in close communion with God. This spiritual immaturity is dangerous because it leaves the person vulnerable to temptation and unprepared for the challenges and responsibilities of the Christian life. The verse from Luke 21:34 is a call to move beyond this shortsightedness, to cultivate a mature faith that looks beyond the immediate and prepares for the eternal.

Moreover, the verse serves as a reminder that life is fleeting, and the time we have to prepare for Christ's return is limited. The Bible teaches that our lives are like a vapor, here today and gone tomorrow. In light of this, it is crucial that we make the most of the time we have, focusing on the things that have eternal significance rather than being consumed by temporary pleasures. Drunkenness, and the shortsightedness that accompanies it, squanders this precious time, leading to a life that is unproductive and unprepared. Jesus' warning in Luke 21:34 is a wake-up call to those who are living for the moment, urging them to shift their focus to the things that truly matter. It is a call to live with the end in mind, to recognize that the choices we make today have eternal consequences, and to ensure that we are ready for Christ's return.

The concept of shortsightedness in this verse also speaks to the broader issue of spiritual awareness. The Bible calls believers to be spiritually alert, to discern the times, and to live in a way that reflects their understanding of God's plan. However, when a person is caught up in drunkenness and the cares of this life, their spiritual senses are dulled. They become unaware of the spiritual realities that surround them, missing the signs of the times and failing to recognize the urgency of the hour. This lack of awareness is dangerous because it leads to complacency, a false sense of security that everything is fine when in reality, the day of the Lord is drawing near. The verse from Luke 21:34 challenges believers to stay spiritually awake, to avoid the distractions and temptations that lead to shortsightedness, and to live in a state of readiness for Christ's return.

In conclusion, Luke 21:34 offers a powerful and urgent warning about the dangers of shortsighted living, particularly when it is marked by drunkenness and an excessive focus on the cares of this life. The verse calls believers to "take heed" to themselves, to be vigilant and self-aware, and to avoid the traps that can lead to spiritual stagnation and unpreparedness. Drunkenness, in particular, is highlighted as a significant danger, as it clouds judgment, dulls spiritual awareness, and leads to a life that is focused on immediate gratification rather than eternal realities. The shortsightedness that comes with such a lifestyle is perilous because it leads to a life that is unprepared for the most important event of all: the return of Christ. The Bible calls believers to live with eternity in mind, to make choices that reflect their faith and their anticipation of Christ's coming. By heeding the warning in Luke 21:34, believers can avoid the pitfalls of shortsightedness, cultivate spiritual maturity, and live lives that are ready for the Lord's return. The dangers of shortsighted living are clear: it leads to a life that is unproductive, unprepared, and disconnected from the spiritual realities that truly matter. The call is to rise above these distractions, to live with purpose and focus, and to ensure that we are ready for the day when Christ returns.

Chapter 17 – The Shameful Strength

Isaiah 5:22, "Woe unto them that are mighty to drink wine, and men of strength to mingle strong drink," offers a powerful and convicting message about the false sense of strength and pride that is often associated with the excessive consumption of alcohol. This verse, delivered through the prophet Isaiah, speaks directly to those who take pride in their ability to drink large amounts of alcohol, viewing it as a sign of strength and prowess. The term "shameful strength" perfectly encapsulates the hollow and destructive nature of this kind of strength—strength that is praised and admired by those who indulge in strong drink but is, in reality, a source of shame and spiritual decay. This verse calls out the tragic irony of glorifying something that ultimately leads to one's downfall, revealing the dangers of placing value on something as fleeting and harmful as the ability to handle large quantities of alcohol.

The phrase "mighty to drink wine" highlights a societal issue where the ability to consume large amounts of alcohol is not only accepted but celebrated. In many cultures, there is a tendency to admire those who can "hold their liquor," as if this ability were a mark of endurance, toughness, or even superiority. This kind of thinking equates the consumption of alcohol with strength, yet it is a distorted and dangerous form of strength that brings about destruction rather than honor. Isaiah's use of the word "woe" is a clear indication of the judgment that is to come upon those who find pride in such things. This "shameful strength" is a false strength, one that leads individuals away from the values that truly matter—self-control, wisdom, and righteousness—and into a life that is increasingly dominated by alcohol and the poor choices that accompany it.

The verse also addresses "men of strength to mingle strong drink," which suggests a deeper level of involvement with alcohol, beyond mere consumption. These are individuals who not only drink but also take pride in mixing and creating strong alcoholic beverages, perhaps reveling in the social status or recognition that this brings them. In today's terms, this could be likened to those who take pride in being mixologists or experts in fine wines and spirits, seeing their expertise and ability to create potent drinks as a form of art or a skill to be admired. However, Isaiah's warning is clear—this too is a form of "shameful strength." It's a strength that is misapplied, focused on something that ultimately leads to harm rather than good. The Bible consistently teaches that true strength is found in self-discipline, in the ability to say no to excess, and in living a life that reflects God's wisdom and commands. The strength to drink or to mix strong drinks is, by contrast, a shallow and dangerous form of strength that leads to personal and communal destruction.

Moreover, the concept of "shameful strength" in this verse highlights the moral and spiritual consequences of glorifying alcohol consumption. Those who are "mighty to drink wine" are often seen as the life of the party, the individuals who can drink others under the table, and who seemingly remain unaffected by the effects of alcohol. However, this ability often masks deeper issues, such as an underlying dependence on alcohol, a lack of self-control, or a desire to escape from reality. The Bible warns against such behaviors because they lead to a life that is out of alignment with God's will. Instead of being a source of true strength, the ability to drink large amounts of alcohol becomes a source of shame, as it pulls individuals further away from the values and principles that God calls them to live by. The "strength" to consume alcohol is, in reality, a weakness—a weakness that leads to poor decisions, damaged relationships, and a life that is increasingly disconnected from God's purpose.

The verse also serves as a critique of societal values that place undue emphasis on the wrong kinds of strength. In many cultures, strength is often associated with physical prowess, the ability to endure pain or hardship, or the capacity to dominate others. In the context of alcohol, this translates into a kind of bravado where drinking large amounts is seen as a testament to one's toughness or masculinity. However, the Bible consistently teaches that true strength is found in humility, in the ability to control one's desires, and in living a life that is pleasing to God. The "shameful strength" described in Isaiah 5:22 is a perversion of these values. It takes something that should be a source of pride—strength—and turns it into something that leads to shame and regret. This verse is a reminder that the qualities we admire and strive for should be those that bring us closer to God, not those that lead us down a path of destruction.

Furthermore, the verse highlights the broader societal impact of glorifying the consumption of alcohol. When a culture celebrates those who are "mighty to drink wine," it creates an environment where excessive drinking is not only accepted but encouraged. This can lead to a range of negative consequences, including increased rates of alcoholism, impaired judgment, and the erosion of moral and ethical standards. The Bible teaches that we are to be a light in the world, reflecting God's love, wisdom, and truth to those around us. However, when we allow ourselves to be caught up in the culture of excessive drinking, we dim that light, becoming part of the problem rather than the solution. The "shameful strength" of those who are praised for their drinking abilities is a reflection of a society that has lost sight of what truly matters, focusing instead on temporary pleasures that ultimately lead to long-term harm.

The idea of "shameful strength" also ties into the concept of self-deception. Those who pride themselves on their ability to drink large amounts of alcohol often deceive themselves into thinking that they are in control, that their drinking is a sign of strength rather than a potential weakness. However, the Bible warns that such self-deception can be spiritually dangerous. The false sense of strength that comes from alcohol consumption can lead individuals to ignore the warning signs of addiction, to rationalize their behavior, and to continue down a path that leads away from God. Isaiah's use of the word "woe" is a wake-up call to those who are caught in this cycle of self-deception, urging them to recognize the truth and to turn away from behaviors that bring shame rather than honor. The verse challenges us to examine our own lives, to consider whether we are placing value on the wrong kinds of strength, and to seek the strength that comes from living in accordance with God's will.

In addition, the verse serves as a reminder that true strength is not about what we can endure physically or how much alcohol we can consume, but about our ability to live a life that reflects God's character.

The Bible teaches that the fruit of the Spirit includes self-control, gentleness, and humility—qualities that are often at odds with the culture of excessive drinking. The "shameful strength" of those who are "mighty to drink wine" is a counterfeit strength, one that leads to pride, arrogance, and ultimately, spiritual downfall. True strength, by contrast, is found in the ability to resist temptation, to make wise choices, and to live in a way that honors God. Isaiah's warning in this verse is a call to reject the false strength of alcohol and to seek the true strength that comes from a life of faith, obedience, and humility.

Moreover, the verse highlights the spiritual consequences of living a life that glorifies alcohol consumption. The Bible teaches that our bodies are temples of the Holy Spirit, and we are called to honor God with our bodies. When we allow alcohol to take control of our lives, we are not honoring God; we are dishonoring Him by placing our own desires above His will. The "shameful strength" of those who are "mighty to drink wine" is a form of idolatry, where alcohol becomes a god that is worshipped and prioritized over everything else. This leads to a life that is increasingly disconnected from God, as the person becomes more focused on satisfying their own desires than on living in a way that pleases God. The verse serves as a stark reminder that the choices we make regarding alcohol have spiritual implications, and that we must be careful not to allow the false strength of alcohol to sever our relationship with God.

In conclusion, Isaiah 5:22 offers a powerful and convicting message about the dangers of glorifying alcohol consumption and the false sense of strength that it can create. The verse warns against the "shameful strength" of those who take pride in their ability to drink large amounts of alcohol, highlighting the moral and spiritual consequences of such behavior. This false strength leads to a life that is increasingly dominated by alcohol, where self-control, wisdom, and righteousness are replaced by pride, arrogance, and spiritual decay. The verse challenges us to reject this counterfeit strength and to seek the true strength that comes from living a life that reflects God's character and values. It also serves as a reminder of the broader societal impact of glorifying alcohol consumption, urging us to be a light in the world and to live in a way that honors God rather than indulging in behaviors that lead to shame and regret. The dangers of alcohol are clear: it leads to a life that is disconnected from God, dominated by self-deception, and ultimately, marked by shame rather than honor. The call is to turn away from the false strength of alcohol and to seek the true strength that comes from a life of faith, obedience, and humility, knowing that this is the only strength that leads to lasting peace, joy, and fulfillment in God's kingdom.

Chapter 18 – The Seduction

Hosea 4:11, "Whoredom and wine and new wine take away the heart," delivers a powerful and sobering message about the dangers of seduction, particularly the way alcohol and immorality work together to lead the heart away from righteousness and devotion to God. The verse, written by the prophet Hosea, highlights how easily the human heart can be seduced by the allure of physical pleasures, symbolized by "whoredom" and "wine," and how these pleasures can ultimately steal the heart away from what truly matters. The term "seduction" is a fitting description of this process, as it implies a gradual and often subtle leading astray, where the heart is enticed by the promise of immediate satisfaction, only to find itself further and further removed from the path of righteousness and spiritual health. This verse underscores the idea that the pleasures of this world, especially when indulged in excess, have a profound ability to corrupt, to lead people away from their values, and to harden their hearts against the things of God.

The phrase "take away the heart" is particularly poignant, as it speaks to the profound impact that sin and excess can have on the innermost part of a person. In biblical language, the heart is not just the seat of emotions, but also the center of one's will, desires, and moral compass. To have one's heart "taken away" suggests a loss of self-control, a surrender of one's moral integrity, and a disconnection from the spiritual truths that should guide one's life. When the heart is seduced by whoredom and wine, it becomes enslaved to desires that are contrary to God's will, leading the person into a life of indulgence, immorality, and ultimately, spiritual death. The seduction of alcohol, in particular, is dangerous because it works subtly, dulling the senses and weakening the resolve, making it easier for other sins to take root in a person's life. The Bible warns repeatedly that those who allow their hearts to be led astray by such pleasures will find themselves on a path that leads to destruction.

Seduction, in the context of this verse, is a process that often begins with small compromises. A person might start by indulging in a little wine or engaging in minor immoral acts, thinking that they can control their behavior and that it will not have a significant impact on their life. However, as the seduction deepens, these small indulgences grow into habits, and the person finds themselves increasingly drawn into a lifestyle of excess and immorality. The heart, once focused on the things of God, becomes consumed with the pursuit of pleasure, and the person becomes blind to the spiritual dangers that are closing in around them. The seductive power of wine and immorality is that they promise satisfaction and fulfillment, but in reality, they lead to emptiness and spiritual decay. The verse from Hosea serves as a stark warning that what may seem like harmless pleasures can quickly become chains that bind the heart and lead it far away from God.

The connection between wine and whoredom in this verse highlights the way that different forms of indulgence often go hand in hand. Alcohol, when consumed in excess, lowers inhibitions and impairs judgment, making it easier for a person to engage in behaviors that they would otherwise avoid. This is why the Bible often warns against drunkenness, not just because of the physical effects of alcohol, but because of the moral and spiritual dangers that come with it. When a person is under the influence of alcohol, they are more likely to make poor decisions, to act impulsively, and to give in to temptations that they would resist when sober. The seduction of wine leads directly into the seduction of immorality, creating a cycle of sin that is difficult to break. The verse from Hosea 4:11 makes it clear that these two forces—wine and immorality—work together to take away the heart, to strip a person of their moral compass, and to lead them into a life that is increasingly distant from God.

The imagery of the heart being "taken away" also speaks to the loss of true love and devotion. The Bible teaches that the greatest commandment is to love the Lord your God with all your heart, soul, mind, and strength. When a person's heart is seduced by wine and immorality, their capacity to love God is diminished. Their affections become divided, with their love for God competing with their love for the pleasures of this world. This divided heart is one of the most tragic consequences of seduction, as it leads to a life that is spiritually lukewarm, half-hearted, and ultimately unfulfilling. The verse from Hosea warns that when the heart is taken away by these seductive forces, it becomes difficult, if not impossible, to fully devote oneself to God. The pleasures of wine and immorality become idols that demand worship, drawing the person's attention, energy, and love away from God and toward things that are temporary and ultimately destructive.

Furthermore, the verse highlights the broader impact of seduction on one's life. When the heart is taken away by wine and immorality, it affects every aspect of a person's being. Their relationships suffer, as they become more focused on satisfying their own desires than on loving and serving others. Their ability to make wise decisions is compromised, as their judgment becomes clouded by the effects of alcohol and the pursuit of pleasure. Their sense of purpose and direction is lost, as they become increasingly consumed by the immediate gratification of their desires rather than the pursuit of long-term, meaningful goals. The Bible teaches that a life centered on God is one of peace, joy, and fulfillment, but when the heart is seduced by the things of this world, these blessings are replaced by turmoil, emptiness, and regret. The verse from Hosea 4:11 is a powerful reminder that the seduction of wine and immorality leads to a life that is out of alignment with God's will and that the consequences of this seduction are far-reaching and devastating.

The idea of seduction also ties into the concept of spiritual warfare. The Bible teaches that believers are engaged in a constant battle against the forces of darkness, which seek to lead them away from God and into sin. Wine and immorality are tools that the enemy uses to seduce believers, to weaken their resolve, and to pull them away from their relationship with God. The seduction is often subtle, beginning with small compromises and gradually leading to a full-scale abandonment of faith and devotion. This is why the Bible repeatedly warns believers to be vigilant, to guard their hearts, and to avoid the things that can lead them astray. The verse from Hosea serves as a call to arms, urging believers to recognize the dangers of seduction and to stand firm against the forces that seek to take away their hearts.

In addition, the verse speaks to the importance of repentance and the need to return to God when one's heart has been led astray. The Bible teaches that God is merciful and that He desires for all people to come to repentance and to be restored to a right relationship with Him. When a person recognizes that their heart has been taken away by wine and immorality, the first step is to repent, to turn away from these seductive forces, and to seek God's forgiveness and healing. The verse from Hosea is a reminder that no one is beyond the reach of God's grace, and that even those who have been deeply seduced by the pleasures of this world can be restored and redeemed. The key is to recognize the seduction for what it is—a lie that promises satisfaction but delivers only emptiness—and to turn back to the source of true life and fulfillment, which is found in God alone.

The verse also challenges believers to examine their own lives and to ask whether they are allowing themselves to be seduced by the things of this world. It is easy to become complacent, to think that a little indulgence in wine or a little compromise in morality is harmless. However, the verse from Hosea warns that even small compromises can lead to a gradual erosion of one's spiritual health. The seduction is often slow and subtle, but it is no less dangerous. The challenge for believers is to remain vigilant, to guard their hearts, and to keep their focus on the things that truly matter—loving God, serving others, and living a life that is pleasing to Him. By doing so, they can avoid the traps of seduction and remain steadfast in their faith.

In conclusion, Hosea 4:11 offers a powerful and sobering message about the dangers of seduction, particularly the way that wine and immorality work together to lead the heart away from God. The verse highlights how easily the human heart can be taken away by the allure of physical pleasures, and how these pleasures can ultimately steal a person's heart, leading them into a life of spiritual darkness and separation from God. The seduction of wine and immorality is dangerous because it is subtle, often beginning with small compromises that gradually grow into habits that dominate a person's life. The verse warns that when the heart is taken away by these seductive forces, it becomes difficult to fully love and serve God, leading to a life that is unfulfilling and out of alignment with His will. The challenge for believers is to recognize the dangers of seduction, to guard their hearts, and to remain steadfast in their faith, avoiding the traps that seek to pull them away from their relationship with God. By doing so, they can live a life that is centered on God, filled with His peace, joy, and fulfillment, and free from the destructive power of seduction.

Chapter 19 – The Stricken

1 Timothy 3:3, "Not given to wine, no striker, not greedy of filthy lucre; but patient, not a brawler, not covetous," provides a critical blueprint for the qualities expected in a leader, particularly within the context of Christian leadership. The verse, penned by the Apostle Paul as guidance for choosing church overseers, underscores the importance of self-control, patience, and moral integrity. One of the key warnings in this verse is against being "given to wine," a phrase that highlights the dangers of alcohol, especially for those in positions of leadership. The term "stricken" perfectly encapsulates the devastating impact that indulgence in alcohol can have on a leader's effectiveness, moral standing, and ability to guide others. To be "stricken" suggests being afflicted or struck down by something powerful and debilitating. In the context of leadership, being stricken with the vice of alcohol consumption can lead to failure, a loss of respect, and ultimately, the downfall of one's ability to lead with integrity and purpose.

The phrase "not given to wine" directly addresses the necessity for leaders to exhibit temperance and self-discipline. Leaders are expected to be examples for others, guiding them not only through their words but through their actions. When a leader is given to wine, they lose their ability to exercise sound judgment, to make wise decisions, and to maintain the kind of composure and clear-mindedness that is essential for effective leadership. Alcohol, when abused, clouds the mind, impairs decision-making, and often leads to behavior that is reckless, irresponsible, or even violent. The Bible warns repeatedly about the dangers of drunkenness, and this verse makes it clear that those who aspire to leadership must avoid being stricken by the temptation of alcohol. A leader who is given to wine is more likely to become a "striker" or a "brawler," engaging in physical or verbal altercations that damage their reputation and undermine their authority. Such behavior is antithetical to the patience and gentleness that are also highlighted in this verse as crucial traits for a leader.

Being stricken with the vice of alcohol can lead to a multitude of failures in leadership. One of the most immediate and visible effects is the loss of respect and trust from those one is supposed to lead. When followers see their leader succumbing to the temptations of alcohol, they may begin to question the leader's judgment, reliability, and commitment to the values they are supposed to uphold. This erosion of trust can be devastating, as it undermines the leader's ability to inspire and guide others. A leader who is stricken with alcohol is also more likely to make decisions that are driven by impulse rather than reason, leading to mistakes that could have been avoided with a clear mind and a sober heart. The Bible emphasizes the importance of wisdom and discernment in leadership, and these qualities are severely compromised when a leader is under the influence of alcohol. The verse from 1 Timothy 3:3 serves as a stark reminder that a leader must remain vigilant, avoiding the pitfalls of alcohol that can so easily lead to failure.

Moreover, being "not given to wine" is not just about avoiding drunkenness; it also reflects a broader commitment to self-control and moderation in all areas of life. A leader who exercises self-control in their consumption of alcohol is likely to exhibit the same discipline in other aspects of their life, such as managing finances, relationships, and responsibilities. This self-control is a cornerstone of effective leadership, as it enables the leader to stay focused on their goals, to resist temptations, and to maintain a steady course even in the face of challenges. On the other hand, a leader who lacks this self-control is more likely to be stricken by the consequences of their actions, whether it's the loss of personal integrity, the breakdown of relationships, or the failure to fulfill their duties. The verse from 1 Timothy 3:3 underscores the idea that leadership is not just about holding a position of authority; it is about living a life that exemplifies the values and principles that one seeks to instill in others.

The warning against being "given to wine" also speaks to the broader cultural and societal implications of alcohol consumption. In many societies, alcohol is often associated with social gatherings, celebrations, and even business dealings. While moderate consumption of alcohol is not inherently sinful, the Bible warns that it can easily become a snare, leading to excess and addiction. For a leader, the stakes are even higher, as their actions are often scrutinized and emulated by others. A leader who is seen indulging in alcohol may inadvertently send the message that such behavior is acceptable, or even desirable, leading others down the same dangerous path. The verse from 1 Timothy 3:3 challenges leaders to set a higher standard, to be mindful of the example they are setting, and to avoid being stricken by the negative consequences of alcohol consumption. This is particularly important in a Christian context, where leaders are called to be representatives of Christ, embodying His teachings and His character in every aspect of their lives.

Furthermore, the verse highlights the interconnectedness of various vices, such as greed, violence, and covetousness, with the consumption of alcohol. A leader who is stricken by one of these vices is more likely to be susceptible to others as well. For example, a leader who is given to wine may also be more prone to greed, as their judgment is impaired and their priorities become skewed. They may seek to satisfy their own desires at the expense of others, leading to unethical decisions and a loss of integrity. Similarly, a leader who is given to wine may become a "striker," using physical force or harsh words to assert their authority or to resolve conflicts. This kind of behavior is destructive, both to the leader's reputation and to the well-being of those they are supposed to lead. The verse from 1 Timothy 3:3 serves as a comprehensive warning against the dangers of these interconnected vices, urging leaders to cultivate virtues such as patience, gentleness, and self-control, which are essential for effective and godly leadership.

The concept of being stricken with failure in leadership due to alcohol also ties into the idea of spiritual warfare. The Bible teaches that believers, and especially leaders, are engaged in a constant battle against the forces of darkness, which seek to lead them astray and to undermine their effectiveness in God's kingdom. Alcohol, when abused, becomes a tool that the enemy uses to weaken leaders, to distract them from their mission, and to cause them to stumble. A leader who is stricken by alcohol is less likely to be vigilant, to discern the enemy's tactics, and to stand firm in the face of spiritual attacks. The verse from 1 Timothy 3:3 reminds leaders of the importance of remaining spiritually strong and alert, avoiding the snares that can lead to failure and ensuring that they are equipped to fulfill the responsibilities that God has entrusted to them.

Additionally, the verse highlights the importance of accountability in leadership. Leaders are not meant to walk alone; they are part of a community of believers who support, encourage, and hold one another accountable. A leader who is stricken by alcohol is likely to isolate themselves, either out of shame or out of a desire to hide their struggles. This isolation only exacerbates the problem, as the leader becomes more vulnerable to temptation and less likely to seek help. The verse from 1 Timothy 3:3 encourages leaders to be open about their struggles, to seek accountability from trusted friends and mentors, and to take proactive steps to avoid being stricken by the dangers of alcohol. By doing so, they can maintain their integrity, stay focused on their mission, and avoid the pitfalls that lead to failure in leadership.

In conclusion, 1 Timothy 3:3 offers a powerful and sobering message about the dangers of being stricken with failure in leadership due to the influence of alcohol. The verse underscores the importance of self-control, patience, and moral integrity in those who aspire to lead, particularly within the context of Christian leadership. A leader who is "given to wine" is more likely to be stricken by the negative consequences of alcohol, including impaired judgment, reckless behavior, and a loss of respect and trust from those they lead. The verse challenges leaders to set a higher standard, to avoid the pitfalls of alcohol, and to cultivate the virtues that are essential for effective and godly leadership. It also serves as a reminder of the interconnectedness of various vices, such as greed, violence, and covetousness, and the importance of remaining vigilant in the face of spiritual warfare. By heeding the warning in 1 Timothy 3:3, leaders can avoid being stricken with failure, maintain their integrity, and fulfill the responsibilities that God has entrusted to them. The dangers of alcohol are clear: it leads to a life that is out of alignment with God's will, marked by poor decisions, damaged relationships, and ultimately, failure in leadership. The call is to turn away from the temptations of alcohol, to seek God's strength and guidance, and to lead with the kind of wisdom, patience, and self-control that reflect God's character and advance His kingdom.

Chapter 20 – The Self-willed

Titus 1:7, "For a bishop must be blameless, as the steward of God; not selfwilled, not soon angry, not given to wine, no striker, not given to filthy lucre," offers profound insight into the qualities required for those in positions of spiritual leadership, particularly highlighting the dangers of being self-willed and how this trait can be exacerbated by the influence of alcohol. The term "self-willed" refers to a person who is stubbornly set on doing things their own way, driven by their own desires, and unwilling to submit to the authority or guidance of others, including God. In the context of leadership, being self-willed is a serious flaw because it means that the leader is more concerned with their own opinions and interests than with the well-being of those they are meant to serve. When this trait is coupled with the consumption of alcohol, it can lead to a toxic combination that not only undermines the leader's effectiveness but also has devastating consequences for the community they are supposed to lead.

The verse begins by stating that a bishop, or overseer, must be "blameless, as the steward of God." This sets a high standard for those in leadership, emphasizing the need for integrity, accountability, and a life that is above reproach. A steward is someone who is entrusted with the care and management of something valuable, and in this case, the bishop is entrusted with the spiritual care of God's people. Being blameless does not mean being perfect, but it does mean living in a way that is consistent with the teachings of Christ, demonstrating the qualities of humility, self-control, and a willingness to put others before oneself. However, when a leader is self-willed, they become focused on their own agenda, pushing their own ideas and desires at the expense of the greater good. This self-willed attitude is often rooted in pride, and when combined with the influence of alcohol, it can lead to poor decision-making, conflict, and ultimately, a failure to fulfill the responsibilities of leadership.

The phrase "not given to wine" in the verse highlights the particular danger that alcohol poses to those who are self-willed. Alcohol has a way of magnifying a person's existing traits, often bringing out the worst in them. For someone who is already inclined to be self-willed, alcohol can lower inhibitions, impair judgment, and lead to behavior that is reckless and destructive. A self-willed leader who is given to wine is more likely to act impulsively, to lash out in anger, and to make decisions based on their own desires rather than what is best for the community. The verse warns that such behavior is incompatible with the role of a bishop, who is called to be a steward of God's people, guiding them with wisdom, patience, and humility. When a leader allows themselves to be led astray by wine, they lose the ability to lead effectively, becoming a source of division and strife rather than a unifying and nurturing presence.

Being self-willed and given to wine can also lead to a lack of accountability in leadership. A self-willed leader is often resistant to feedback or correction, believing that they know best and that their way is the right way. This attitude can create a toxic environment where the leader becomes isolated, unwilling to listen to others or to seek counsel. Alcohol can further exacerbate this isolation, as the leader may turn to drinking as a way to cope with stress, to escape from the pressures of leadership, or to reinforce their own sense of superiority. The Bible teaches that leaders are meant to be servants, putting the needs of others before their own and seeking to lead by example. However, a self-willed leader who is given to wine is more likely to focus on their own comfort and pleasure, neglecting their responsibilities and failing to provide the kind of leadership that the community needs. The verse from Titus 1:7 serves as a stark reminder that such behavior is unacceptable for those who are called to be stewards of God's people.

Moreover, the verse highlights the importance of self-control in leadership. A leader who is self-willed and given to wine lacks the self-control necessary to lead effectively. Self-control is a fruit of the Spirit, a quality that enables a person to resist temptation, to remain calm in the face of adversity, and to make decisions that are in line with God's will. When a leader is given to wine, they lose this self-control, becoming more prone to anger, impulsivity, and actions that are harmful to themselves and others. The Bible teaches that self-control is essential for living a life that is pleasing to God, and this is especially true for those in leadership. A self-willed leader who lacks self-control is like a ship without a rudder, drifting aimlessly and vulnerable to being tossed about by the waves of their own desires and the pressures of the world. The verse from Titus 1:7 emphasizes that such a leader is unfit to be a steward of God's people, as they are unable to provide the steady, wise, and compassionate guidance that is required.

The verse also speaks to the broader consequences of having a self-willed leader who is given to wine. Such a leader can cause significant harm to the community they are supposed to serve. Instead of fostering a spirit of unity, cooperation, and mutual support, a self-willed leader may create an environment of division, conflict, and mistrust. Their decisions may be driven more by their own interests than by the needs of the community, leading to resentment and disillusionment among those they are supposed to lead. Additionally, the leader's behavior may set a poor example for others, encouraging a culture of excess, indulgence, and self-centeredness. The Bible teaches that leaders are meant to be examples to the flock, living lives that reflect the character of Christ and inspiring others to do the same. However, a self-willed leader who is given to wine fails in this responsibility, leading others astray and undermining the spiritual health of the community.

Furthermore, the verse underscores the importance of humility in leadership. A self-willed leader is often driven by pride, believing that they are always right and that their way is the best way. This pride can make it difficult for the leader to admit when they are wrong, to seek forgiveness, or to make changes that would benefit the community. When combined with alcohol, this pride can become even more pronounced, leading to stubbornness, arrogance, and a refusal to listen to others. The Bible teaches that God opposes the proud but gives grace to the humble, and this is especially true in leadership. A leader who is humble is willing to listen to others, to seek counsel, and to put the needs of the community before their own. By contrast, a self-willed leader who is given to wine is more likely to alienate others, to make decisions that are harmful, and to ultimately fail in their role as a steward of God's people. The verse from Titus 1:7 calls for leaders who are humble, who recognize their own limitations, and who are willing to submit to God's will rather than their own.

In addition, the verse serves as a reminder of the responsibility that comes with leadership. A leader is not just responsible for their own actions, but also for the well-being of those they lead. This responsibility requires a high level of integrity, self-discipline, and a commitment to living in a way that honors God. When a leader is self-willed and given to wine, they are shirking this responsibility, putting their own desires ahead of the needs of the community. This can lead to a breakdown in trust, a loss of credibility, and a failure to fulfill the duties of leadership. The verse from Titus 1:7 emphasizes that those who are called to be stewards of God's people must be blameless, not given to wine, and not self-willed. These qualities are essential for effective leadership, as they enable the leader to provide the kind of guidance, support, and example that the community needs.

The concept of being self-willed also ties into the idea of accountability. A self-willed leader may resist accountability, believing that they do not need to answer to anyone else. This attitude can be dangerous, as it can lead to a lack of transparency, a refusal to accept feedback, and a failure to recognize and address one's own shortcomings. The Bible teaches that leaders are accountable to God and to the community they serve, and that they must be willing to submit to the authority of others. A self-willed leader who is given to wine is more likely to reject this accountability, to isolate themselves, and to make decisions that are driven by their own desires rather than by the needs of the community. The verse from Titus 1:7 calls for leaders who are willing to be accountable, who recognize their own limitations, and who are committed to living in a way that reflects the character of Christ.

In conclusion, Titus 1:7 offers a powerful and sobering message about the dangers of being self-willed and how this trait, when combined with the influence of alcohol, can lead to failure in leadership. The verse emphasizes the importance of being blameless, self-controlled, and humble in order to fulfill the responsibilities of a steward of God's people. A self-willed leader who is given to wine is likely to be led astray, making decisions that are driven by their own desires rather than by the needs of the community. This can lead to a breakdown in trust, a loss of credibility, and a failure to provide the kind of guidance and support that the community needs. The verse calls for leaders who are willing to submit to God's will, to seek accountability, and to live in a way that reflects the character of Christ. By heeding this warning, leaders can avoid the pitfalls of being self-willed and given to wine, and instead provide the kind of leadership that is blameless, compassionate, and effective in advancing God's kingdom. The dangers of being self-willed and given to wine are clear: they lead to a life that is out of alignment with God's will, marked by poor decisions, damaged relationships, and ultimately, failure in leadership. The call is to turn away from these temptations, to seek God's strength and guidance, and to lead with the kind of wisdom, patience, and humility that reflect God's character and advance His kingdom.

Chapter 21 – The Sacrilege

Leviticus 10:9, "Do not drink wine nor strong drink, thou, nor thy sons with thee, when ye go into the tabernacle of the congregation, lest ye die: it shall be a statute for ever throughout your generations," delivers a powerful and solemn warning about the dangers of mixing alcohol with worship, highlighting the sacrilegious nature of such an act. This verse, spoken by God to Aaron and his sons, establishes a strict prohibition against consuming alcohol before entering the tabernacle, the sacred place where the Israelites worshiped and met with God. The term "sacrilege" perfectly encapsulates the gravity of the offense committed when someone approaches God's holy presence under the influence of alcohol. To commit sacrilege is to violate or profane something that is sacred, and in this context, it means to dishonor the sanctity of worship by allowing one's mind and body to be compromised by alcohol. The warning in Leviticus 10:9 is clear and severe: those who drink wine or strong drink before coming into the tabernacle risk death, underscoring the seriousness with which God views the purity and reverence required in His presence.

The context of this verse is significant, as it follows the tragic account of Nadab and Abihu, Aaron's sons, who offered "strange fire" before the Lord and were consumed by fire as a result of their disobedience (Leviticus 10:1-2). Although the Bible does not explicitly state that alcohol was involved in their transgression, the immediate command from God to Aaron and his remaining sons to abstain from wine and strong drink before entering the tabernacle suggests that intoxication may have contributed to their fatal mistake. This connection between alcohol and the failure to properly conduct worship highlights the dangers of sacrilege, where the mind-altering effects of alcohol can lead to actions that are irreverent, careless, and ultimately deadly in the presence of a holy God. The verse serves as a stark reminder that worship is not a casual activity, but a sacred duty that requires full awareness, self-control, and a deep respect for God's holiness.

The prohibition against drinking alcohol before worship is rooted in the need for clarity of mind and purity of heart when approaching God. The tabernacle was the dwelling place of God's presence among the Israelites, and those who served there, particularly the priests, were required to maintain the highest standards of holiness and reverence. Alcohol, with its ability to impair judgment, dull the senses, and lower inhibitions, poses a direct threat to these standards. A priest who is under the influence of alcohol is not in a fit state to perform the sacred duties required in the tabernacle, whether it be offering sacrifices, burning incense, or making intercessions on behalf of the people. The verse from Leviticus 10:9 emphasizes that approaching God with anything less than full mental and spiritual clarity is not only disrespectful but dangerous, as it exposes the individual to the risk of divine judgment. This commandment was not just a temporary rule for the priests of that time, but a "statute for ever throughout your generations," indicating its lasting importance and relevance.

The concept of sacrilege, as described in this verse, extends beyond the specific act of drinking alcohol before worship; it speaks to the broader issue of how one approaches God in worship. Worship is meant to be an expression of reverence, adoration, and submission to God. It is a time when believers set aside the distractions and concerns of the world to focus solely on God's greatness, holiness, and love. However, when someone comes to worship under the influence of alcohol, they are not fully present in mind, body, or spirit. Their ability to engage with God is compromised, and their worship becomes tainted by the influence of a substance that has no place in the holy presence of God. This is the essence of sacrilege—when the sacred act of worship is defiled by something that should not be there, something that diminishes the honor and glory that is due to God alone.

The dangers of sacrilege are not limited to the individual who commits it; they have broader implications for the community of believers as well. In the context of the Israelites, the priests served as intermediaries between God and the people, and their actions in the tabernacle had a direct impact on the entire nation. If a priest approached the altar under the influence of alcohol and performed his duties carelessly or incorrectly, the consequences could be disastrous, not just for him but for the entire congregation. This is why the command in Leviticus 10:9 is so stringent and why the penalty for disobedience is so severe. The holiness of God and the integrity of worship must be preserved at all costs, for the sake of both the individual and the community. The Bible teaches that the worship of God is a communal activity, where the people of God come together to honor Him, to receive His blessings, and to be shaped by His presence. When sacrilege occurs, it disrupts this sacred exchange, bringing dishonor to God and potentially leading to spiritual harm for the entire community.

The verse also highlights the importance of discipline and self-control in the life of a believer, particularly in the context of worship. The command to abstain from alcohol before entering the tabernacle is a call to maintain a state of readiness and alertness when coming into God's presence. Worship is not something to be approached lightly or casually; it requires preparation, focus, and a deep sense of reverence. Alcohol, with its ability to impair these qualities, has no place in the life of a worshiper who seeks to honor God with all their heart, soul, mind, and strength. The discipline of abstaining from alcohol before worship is a practical way of ensuring that one's mind is clear, one's heart is pure, and one's spirit is fully attuned to the presence of God. This discipline reflects a broader principle in the Christian life: the need to be vigilant and self-controlled in all things, avoiding anything that could hinder one's relationship with God or one's ability to worship Him in spirit and truth.

Furthermore, the verse speaks to the enduring relevance of God's commandments concerning worship. The phrase "it shall be a statute for ever throughout your generations" indicates that this commandment was not just for the priests of Aaron's time, but for all who would come after them. While the specific practices of worship may have changed over the centuries, the underlying principles of reverence, holiness, and self-control remain the same. The prohibition against drinking alcohol before worship is a reminder that the standards God sets for His people are not arbitrary or temporary; they are rooted in His unchanging nature and His desire for His people to approach Him with the respect and honor that He deserves. This verse challenges believers to consider how they approach worship today, to examine whether there are any influences—whether it be alcohol, distractions, or unconfessed sin—that might be compromising their ability to worship God fully and faithfully.

The concept of sacrilege also extends to the broader issue of how believers live their lives outside of formal worship. The Bible teaches that worship is not confined to a specific time or place, but is a way of life—a continuous offering of oneself to God in everything one does. This means that the principles of reverence, self-control, and holiness that apply to worship in the tabernacle also apply to the way believers conduct themselves in their daily lives. A believer who is given to alcohol or other substances that impair judgment and self-control is at risk of committing sacrilege, not just in the context of formal worship, but in their everyday actions and decisions. The verse from Leviticus 10:9 challenges believers to live lives that are consistent with the holiness of God, to avoid anything that could lead to sacrilege, and to strive for a purity of heart and mind that honors God in all things.

In conclusion, Leviticus 10:9 delivers a powerful and solemn warning about the dangers of sacrilege, particularly in the context of mixing alcohol with worship. The verse establishes a strict prohibition against drinking wine or strong drink before entering the tabernacle, highlighting the serious consequences of approaching God's holy presence under the influence of alcohol. The term "sacrilege" perfectly captures the gravity of the offense committed when worship is defiled by the presence of alcohol, and the verse serves as a stark reminder that worship requires full mental and spiritual clarity, self-control, and a deep respect for God's holiness. This commandment, given to Aaron and his sons, emphasizes the need for discipline and vigilance in the life of a believer, both in the context of formal worship and in everyday life. The dangers of sacrilege are not limited to the individual who commits it, but have broader implications for the entire community of believers, as the integrity of worship and the honor of God must be preserved at all costs. The verse challenges believers to examine how they approach worship today, to consider whether there are any influences that might be compromising their ability to worship God fully and faithfully, and to strive for a life that is consistent with the holiness of God in all things. By heeding this warning, believers can avoid the pitfalls of sacrilege, maintain the integrity of their worship, and live lives that honor God in every aspect. The call is to turn away from anything that could lead to sacrilege, to seek God's strength and guidance, and to approach worship with the reverence, self-control, and holiness that reflect the character of God and advance His kingdom.

Chapter 22 – The Shortsighted Plans

Isaiah 56:12, "Come ye, say they, I will fetch wine, and we will fill ourselves with strong drink; and to morrow shall be as this day, and much more abundant," is a powerful indictment of the shortsighted plans that often characterize a life given to alcohol. This verse captures the mindset of those who are caught in the cycle of drinking, where the focus is solely on immediate gratification without any regard for the future or the consequences of their actions. The phrase "shortsighted plans" perfectly encapsulates this attitude, where the temporary pleasure of today blinds individuals to the realities of tomorrow. The people in this verse are depicted as living for the moment, indulging in wine and strong drink, with a careless and misplaced confidence that tomorrow will simply bring more of the same, perhaps even in greater abundance. This kind of thinking is not only naive but also dangerous, as it ignores the inevitable consequences of a life dominated by alcohol and the false sense of security it brings.

The shortsightedness described in this verse reveals a deep flaw in the way these individuals perceive life and their place in it. They are so consumed with the present moment and the pleasures that drinking offers that they fail to consider the impact of their choices on their future. The assumption that "tomorrow shall be as this day, and much more abundant" is a classic example of wishful thinking, where individuals deceive themselves into believing that their current lifestyle can continue indefinitely without any repercussions. However, the Bible repeatedly warns that such a mindset is foolish and leads to ruin. The temporary pleasure of alcohol may seem satisfying in the moment, but it often masks deeper issues, such as an inability to cope with life's challenges, a refusal to take responsibility, or a denial of the realities of one's circumstances. By focusing solely on the immediate gratification that alcohol provides, these individuals are setting themselves up for failure, as they neglect to plan for the future, address their underlying problems, or seek out more meaningful and lasting sources of fulfillment.

The verse also highlights the deceptive nature of alcohol, which can create a false sense of security and invincibility. When people are under the influence of alcohol, their perception of reality is often distorted, leading them to believe that they are in control, that their problems are manageable, and that the future will take care of itself. This is why they can make statements like "to morrow shall be as this day, and much more abundant" with such confidence. However, this is a dangerous illusion. Alcohol may temporarily numb pain or provide a sense of euphoria, but it does not solve problems or improve one's circumstances. In fact, it often exacerbates issues, leading to poor decision-making, damaged relationships, and a downward spiral of self-destructive behavior. The shortsighted plans of those who are given to drink are based on a faulty premise, as they rely on alcohol to sustain them rather than facing the realities of their lives and making responsible choices.

Furthermore, the verse illustrates the cyclical nature of a life given to alcohol. The people in this verse are not just drinking to enjoy the present moment; they are planning to continue this behavior into the future, with the expectation that each day will bring more of the same. This creates a vicious cycle where alcohol becomes the central focus of their lives, dictating their plans, decisions, and actions. Instead of pursuing meaningful goals, building healthy relationships, or contributing to society, they are trapped in a cycle of consumption and escapism. This shortsightedness prevents them from seeing the long-term consequences of their actions, such as deteriorating health, broken relationships, financial instability, and spiritual emptiness. The Bible teaches that life is a precious gift, meant to be lived with purpose, wisdom, and a focus on eternal values. However, when individuals are consumed by alcohol, they squander this gift, choosing instead to live in a way that is ultimately unfulfilling and destructive.

The verse also serves as a critique of the complacency and apathy that often accompany a life given to drink. The people in this verse are not just shortsighted; they are also content with their current situation, believing that there is no need for change or improvement. This complacency is reflected in their assumption that "tomorrow shall be as this day," suggesting that they see no need to strive for anything more or to address any challenges that may arise. This attitude is dangerous because it prevents growth, self-improvement, and the pursuit of a better life. The Bible encourages believers to be vigilant, to live with a sense of purpose, and to constantly seek to grow in wisdom, character, and faith. However, a life given to alcohol fosters the opposite mindset, where individuals become stagnant, unmotivated, and unwilling to take the steps necessary to improve their lives. The shortsighted plans that arise from this mindset lead to a life that is marked by missed opportunities, unfulfilled potential, and a lack of true meaning.

Moreover, the verse highlights the contrast between the temporary, fleeting pleasures of alcohol and the lasting, meaningful fulfillment that comes from living a life aligned with God's will. The people in this verse are seeking satisfaction in wine and strong drink, believing that these substances can provide them with happiness and abundance. However, the Bible teaches that true joy and fulfillment come not from the pleasures of this world, but from a relationship with God, living according to His principles, and serving others. The shortsightedness of those who are given to drink prevents them from seeing this truth, as they are blinded by their pursuit of immediate gratification. This leads them to place their trust in something that is ultimately unreliable and insufficient to meet their deepest needs. The verse serves as a reminder that the pursuit of worldly pleasures, particularly through alcohol, is a dead-end path that leads to disappointment, emptiness, and spiritual decay.

The verse also speaks to the broader societal implications of a culture that promotes and glorifies alcohol consumption. When individuals are encouraged to prioritize drinking and to view it as a central part of their social life, it fosters a shortsighted mindset that values immediate pleasure over long-term well-being. This cultural attitude can lead to widespread problems, such as increased rates of alcoholism, broken families, and a general decline in moral and ethical standards. The Bible calls believers to be a light in the world, to live in a way that reflects God's truth and love, and to set an example for others to follow. However, when a culture is dominated by the pursuit of alcohol, it becomes more difficult for individuals to live according to these principles. The verse from Isaiah 56:12 challenges believers to resist the pull of this culture, to avoid the shortsighted plans that arise from a life given to drink, and to pursue a life that is marked by wisdom, self-control, and a focus on what truly matters.

In addition, the verse underscores the importance of planning for the future with wisdom and foresight. The people in this verse are so focused on the present moment that they fail to consider the long-term consequences of their actions. This shortsightedness is a common theme in the Bible, where individuals who prioritize immediate gratification often find themselves facing negative outcomes in the future. The Bible teaches that wisdom involves looking beyond the present moment, considering the potential consequences of one's actions, and making decisions that will lead to long-term success and fulfillment. However, when individuals are given to alcohol, their ability to think clearly and plan effectively is compromised. They become more likely to make impulsive decisions, to neglect important responsibilities, and to overlook the steps necessary to achieve their goals. The verse from Isaiah 56:12 serves as a warning that a life dominated by alcohol leads to shortsighted plans that ultimately result in failure and regret.

The verse also challenges individuals to consider the impact of their choices on others. The people in this verse are focused solely on their own pleasure, with no regard for how their actions might affect those around them. This self-centered attitude is a hallmark of a life given to drink, where the pursuit of alcohol often takes precedence over relationships, responsibilities, and the well-being of others. The Bible teaches that believers are called to love their neighbors, to serve others, and to live in a way that reflects God's love and compassion. However, when individuals are consumed by alcohol, they become more likely to neglect these responsibilities, to hurt those they care about, and to create a ripple effect of negative consequences in their communities. The verse from Isaiah 56:12 challenges individuals to move beyond shortsighted, self-centered plans and to consider how their actions align with their calling to love and serve others.

In conclusion, Isaiah 56:12 offers a powerful and convicting message about the dangers of shortsighted plans that arise from a life given to alcohol. The verse captures the mindset of those who are caught in the cycle of drinking, where the focus is solely on immediate gratification without any regard for the future or the consequences of their actions. This shortsightedness leads to a life that is marked by missed opportunities, unfulfilled potential, and a lack of true meaning. The verse warns that the temporary pleasure of alcohol creates a false sense of security, blinding individuals to the realities of their circumstances and leading them down a path of self-destruction. The cyclical nature of alcohol consumption traps individuals in a cycle of consumption and escapism, preventing them from pursuing meaningful goals, building healthy relationships, or contributing to society. The verse challenges individuals to resist the pull of a culture that promotes alcohol, to avoid the shortsighted plans that arise from a life given to drink, and to pursue a life that is marked by wisdom, self-control, and a focus on what truly matters. It also underscores the importance of planning for the future with wisdom and foresight, considering the impact of one's choices on others, and living in a way that reflects God's love and compassion. By heeding this warning, individuals can avoid the pitfalls of shortsighted plans, live lives that are aligned with God's will, and experience the lasting fulfillment that comes from a life dedicated to serving God and others. The call is to turn away from the temporary, fleeting pleasures of alcohol, to seek the wisdom and guidance of God, and to live with a focus on the future, on eternal values, and on the relationships that truly matter.

Chapter 23 – The Squandered Potential

Proverbs 23:20-21, "Be not among winebibbers; among riotous eaters of flesh: For the drunkard and the glutton shall come to poverty: and drowsiness shall clothe a man with rags," provides a powerful and sobering reflection on the consequences of indulgence in alcohol and gluttony, highlighting how such behaviors lead to a life marked by squandered potential. The term "squandered potential" perfectly encapsulates the tragic reality that unfolds when a person allows themselves to be consumed by the fleeting pleasures of drunkenness and excessive eating. This verse, rich in wisdom, serves as a stern warning that the pursuit of immediate gratification, especially through alcohol, often results in the erosion of one's future prospects, talents, and opportunities. The imagery used—drunkenness leading to poverty, and drowsiness clothing a person with rags—paints a vivid picture of a life that could have been full of promise and achievement, but instead ends in destitution and despair because of poor choices and lack of self-control.

At the heart of this warning is the understanding that every individual is endowed with unique talents, abilities, and opportunities that, when properly nurtured and directed, can lead to a life of purpose, fulfillment, and success. However, when a person chooses to indulge in behaviors like drunkenness and gluttony, they are essentially trading these long-term rewards for short-lived pleasures. The verse warns against keeping company with "winebibbers" and "riotous eaters of flesh," emphasizing that such associations can pull a person into a lifestyle that is focused on immediate sensory satisfaction rather than on building a meaningful and productive life. This kind of lifestyle is inherently self-destructive because it prioritizes momentary pleasure over long-term well-being. The Bible consistently teaches that wisdom involves looking beyond the present moment, making decisions that are in line with one's future goals and responsibilities. However, when a person is caught up in the cycle of drinking and indulgence, their ability to make wise, forward-thinking decisions is compromised, leading to a gradual but inevitable decline in their circumstances and prospects.

The phrase "the drunkard and the glutton shall come to poverty" highlights the direct connection between these indulgent behaviors and the material consequences that follow. Poverty, in this context, is not just a lack of financial resources, but also a deeper impoverishment of the soul, the mind, and one's potential. A person who spends their time and resources on alcohol and excess is squandering the very assets—both material and immaterial—that could have been used to build a stable, successful, and fulfilling life. This kind of poverty is insidious because it often creeps up gradually; a person may not realize the extent of the damage until it is too late. The verse from Proverbs serves as a wake-up call, urging individuals to recognize the long-term consequences of their actions and to steer clear of the path that leads to such a tragic outcome.

The mention of "drowsiness" in the verse adds another layer of meaning to the warning. Drowsiness, in this context, symbolizes a state of laziness, neglect, and inattention to one's duties and responsibilities. It is the natural consequence of a lifestyle centered around excessive drinking and eating, where the pursuit of pleasure takes precedence over the pursuit of meaningful work, growth, and personal development. A person who is constantly in a state of drowsiness due to their indulgent habits is unable to fully engage with the opportunities and challenges that life presents. They become lethargic, unmotivated, and increasingly disconnected from their own potential. The phrase "drowsiness shall clothe a man with rags" is a powerful metaphor for the degradation that occurs when a person fails to take care of themselves and their responsibilities. The rags represent the deterioration of one's life and prospects, the visible signs of a life that has been wasted through poor choices and lack of discipline.

Moreover, the verse from Proverbs 23:20-21 highlights the importance of choosing one's companions wisely. The admonition to "be not among winebibbers; among riotous eaters of flesh" underscores the influence that our social circles can have on our behavior and decisions. Associating with those who prioritize indulgence in alcohol and food over more meaningful pursuits can easily lead to a person adopting the same habits and attitudes. The Bible teaches that "bad company corrupts good character," and this is particularly true when it comes to behaviors that involve excess and lack of self-control. By surrounding themselves with people who are focused on short-term pleasures, an individual is more likely to adopt the same mindset, leading to a gradual erosion of their own values, goals, and potential. The verse serves as a reminder to be mindful of the company we keep and to seek out relationships that encourage growth, responsibility, and a focus on long-term success and fulfillment.

The concept of squandered potential also extends to the spiritual realm. The Bible teaches that each person is created in the image of God, with a unique purpose and calling. When a person allows themselves to be consumed by alcohol and indulgence, they are not only squandering their material resources but also neglecting the spiritual gifts and opportunities that God has given them. This neglect can lead to a sense of spiritual emptiness and dissatisfaction, as the person becomes increasingly disconnected from their true purpose and calling. The verse from Proverbs 23:20-21 serves as a reminder that our lives are meant to be lived in a way that honors God and reflects His love, wisdom, and grace. When we choose to focus on short-term pleasures instead of seeking God's will for our lives, we are squandering the incredible potential that God has placed within us. This spiritual impoverishment is perhaps the most tragic consequence of all, as it affects not only our lives on earth but also our eternal destiny.

Furthermore, the verse challenges us to consider the broader impact of our choices on those around us. The behaviors of drunkenness and gluttony are often portrayed as personal choices that affect only the individual, but in reality, they can have far-reaching consequences for families, communities, and even society as a whole. A person who is consumed by these behaviors is less likely to contribute positively to their community, to fulfill their responsibilities to their family, or to be a source of support and encouragement to others. Instead, they may become a burden, relying on others to pick up the pieces of their life and to provide the care and resources that they are no longer able to provide for themselves. The verse from Proverbs 23:20-21 reminds us that our choices do not exist in a vacuum; they have a ripple effect that can impact the lives of those around us in profound ways. By choosing a path of wisdom, self-control, and responsibility, we not only preserve our own potential but also contribute to the well-being and flourishing of others.

The verse also speaks to the importance of discipline and self-control in achieving one's goals and fulfilling one's potential. The Bible consistently teaches that self-discipline is a key component of a successful and meaningful life. It enables us to resist temptations, to stay focused on our goals, and to persevere in the face of challenges. When a person lacks self-discipline, they are more likely to give in to the temptations of alcohol and indulgence, leading to a life that is marked by missed opportunities and unfulfilled potential. The verse from Proverbs 23:20-21 serves as a call to cultivate the discipline needed to avoid the pitfalls of excess and to stay focused on the things that truly matter. This discipline is not just about avoiding negative behaviors, but also about actively pursuing the habits and practices that lead to growth, success, and fulfillment.

In addition, the verse encourages us to reflect on the legacy we are leaving behind. The choices we make today, particularly those related to our habits and behaviors, have a lasting impact on our future and on the legacy we leave for others. A life marked by drunkenness and indulgence is unlikely to leave a positive legacy; instead, it may be remembered for its wasted potential and the opportunities that were lost along the way. The Bible teaches that we are called to live lives that make a positive impact on the world, to leave behind a legacy of faith, love, and good works. The verse from Proverbs 23:20-21 challenges us to consider whether our current choices are helping us to build that kind of legacy or whether they are leading us down a path of squandered potential and regret.

The verse also serves as a reminder of the importance of living with a sense of purpose and direction. When a person is consumed by alcohol and indulgence, they are often living without a clear sense of purpose or direction. Their focus is on the immediate gratification of their desires, rather than on the pursuit of meaningful goals or the fulfillment of their potential. The Bible teaches that our lives are meant to be lived with purpose, guided by the principles and values that God has given us. When we lose sight of that purpose, we are more likely to make choices that lead to a life of squandered potential. The verse from Proverbs 23:20-21 encourages us to stay focused on our purpose, to make decisions that align with our values and goals, and to avoid the distractions and temptations that can lead us astray.

In conclusion, Proverbs 23:20-21 offers a powerful and sobering warning about the dangers of squandered potential that result from a life given to alcohol and indulgence. The verse highlights the direct connection between these behaviors and the material, spiritual, and relational consequences that follow. It challenges us to recognize the long-term impact of our choices, to cultivate the discipline and self-control needed to avoid the pitfalls of excess, and to stay focused on the things that truly matter in life. The verse also encourages us to reflect on the legacy we are leaving behind, to consider the impact of our choices on those around us, and to live with a sense of purpose and direction. By heeding this warning, we can

avoid the tragic consequences of squandered potential, preserve the gifts and opportunities that God has given us, and build a life that is marked by growth, success, and fulfillment. The call is to turn away from the temporary pleasures of alcohol and indulgence, to seek the wisdom and guidance of God, and to live a life that honors Him and reflects His love, wisdom, and grace.

Chapter 24 – The Sleepiness

1 Thessalonians 5:7, "For they that sleep sleep in the night; and they that be drunken are drunken in the night," provides a profound insight into the dangers of spiritual sleepiness that often accompanies indulgence in alcohol. This verse, written by the Apostle Paul, serves as a stark warning about the consequences of allowing oneself to be lulled into a state of spiritual lethargy and unawareness through the consumption of alcohol. The term "sleepiness" in this context goes beyond mere physical drowsiness; it represents a deeper, more dangerous state of spiritual unawareness and neglect. When individuals give themselves over to drinking, particularly in excess, they are not just numbing their physical senses, but they are also dulling their spiritual alertness, becoming increasingly insensitive to the movements of God, the needs of others, and the moral responsibilities they bear. This kind of sleepiness is particularly insidious because it can creep up slowly, unnoticed at first, but eventually envelops a person entirely, leaving them vulnerable to the many dangers that lurk in the spiritual darkness of the night.

The metaphor of "night" in this verse is significant because it symbolizes a time of darkness, not only in the literal sense but also in the spiritual sense. Nighttime is traditionally associated with danger, uncertainty, and the absence of light. In the Bible, light often represents truth, wisdom, and the presence of God, while darkness symbolizes ignorance, sin, and separation from God. When Paul speaks of those who "sleep in the night" and "are drunken in the night," he is painting a picture of people who are spiritually disconnected, living in a state of moral and spiritual darkness. They are not awake to the realities of their situation; they are not vigilant or prepared for what lies ahead. Instead, they are caught up in the temporary, fleeting pleasures of the moment, allowing themselves to be consumed by the false comfort that alcohol provides. This kind of sleepiness is dangerous because it leaves a person unprepared for the challenges and trials that are sure to come, as well as the ultimate return of Christ, which the Bible teaches could happen at any moment.

The connection between drunkenness and spiritual sleepiness is particularly poignant because alcohol has the ability to dull not only the physical senses but also the spiritual senses. When a person is under the influence of alcohol, their ability to think clearly, to make sound decisions, and to discern right from wrong is compromised. This state of impairment is not limited to the mind and body; it also affects the soul. A person who indulges in alcohol, especially in excess, is less likely to engage in spiritual practices such as prayer, meditation, or reading Scripture. They become more focused on satisfying their immediate desires and less concerned with their spiritual well-being. Over time, this leads to a kind of spiritual sleepiness, where the individual becomes increasingly detached from their faith, from God, and from the community of believers. They are no longer actively pursuing a relationship with God or seeking to grow in their faith; instead, they are drifting, spiritually asleep, and unaware of the dangers that surround them.

This spiritual sleepiness is particularly dangerous because it often goes unnoticed by the person who is experiencing it. Just as physical sleep can come upon a person gradually, so too can spiritual sleepiness. It starts with small compromises—perhaps a drink here and there, a decision to skip church or prayer, a growing focus on worldly pleasures rather than on spiritual growth. These small choices add up over time, leading to a state of spiritual drowsiness where the individual is no longer fully engaged in their faith. They may still go through the motions—attending church, participating in religious activities—but their heart is no longer fully in it. They are spiritually asleep, unaware of how far they have drifted from the vibrant, active faith they once had. This is why the Bible repeatedly warns believers to be vigilant, to stay awake, and to be sober-minded, especially in the face of temptations like alcohol, which can so easily lead to spiritual lethargy and eventual downfall.

Moreover, the verse from 1 Thessalonians 5:7 highlights the contrast between those who live in the light and those who live in the darkness. The Bible teaches that believers are called to be children of the light, living in a way that reflects the truth, wisdom, and holiness of God. This requires a constant state of vigilance, self-control, and spiritual alertness. However, those who indulge in alcohol and allow themselves to become spiritually sleepy are living in the darkness, disconnected from the light of God's truth. They are not prepared for the challenges and trials that are sure to come, nor are they ready for the return of Christ. The verse serves as a reminder that the Christian life is not one of complacency or indulgence, but one of active engagement, constant growth, and readiness. To fall into spiritual sleepiness is to risk being caught unprepared when the day of the Lord arrives, a day that the Bible teaches will come like a thief in the night, suddenly and without warning.

The concept of spiritual sleepiness also speaks to the broader issue of how we live our daily lives. The Bible teaches that every aspect of our lives—our thoughts, words, actions, and habits—should be oriented toward God and His purposes. When we allow ourselves to be consumed by alcohol, we are essentially choosing to turn away from this God-centered way of living and instead embracing a life that is focused on self-gratification. This shift in focus leads to a kind of spiritual inertia, where we become less motivated to pursue the things of God and more likely to settle for a life of complacency. The verse from 1 Thessalonians 5:7 challenges us to examine our own lives and to ask whether we are living in a state of spiritual wakefulness or whether we have allowed ourselves to become spiritually sleepy, lulled into a false sense of security by the temporary pleasures of this world.

Furthermore, the verse serves as a warning about the dangers of peer influence and societal norms. In many cultures, alcohol consumption is not only accepted but often encouraged as a means of relaxation, socialization, or even as a way to cope with stress. However, the Bible calls believers to be set apart from the world, to live according to a different set of values and standards. When we allow ourselves to be influenced by the world's attitudes toward alcohol, we are at risk of becoming spiritually sleepy, gradually adopting behaviors and mindsets that are contrary to our faith. The verse from 1 Thessalonians 5:7 reminds us that we are called to live in the light, to be sober-minded, and to remain vigilant in our walk with God. This means resisting the pressures and temptations of the world and instead choosing to live in a way that is pleasing to God, fully awake and alert to the spiritual realities that surround us.

The concept of sleepiness also extends to the issue of spiritual warfare. The Bible teaches that believers are engaged in a constant battle against the forces of darkness, and that the enemy is always seeking to lead us astray, to dull our senses, and to pull us away from God. Alcohol, when abused, becomes a powerful tool in the enemy's hands, leading us into a state of spiritual sleepiness where we are less able to resist temptation, less aware of the enemy's schemes, and less prepared to stand firm in our faith. The verse from 1 Thessalonians 5:7 serves as a call to arms, urging believers to stay awake, to be vigilant, and to remain sober-minded so that we can effectively engage in this spiritual battle. To fall into spiritual sleepiness is to risk being caught off guard, unprepared to face the challenges and trials that come our way, and ultimately, unprepared to meet the Lord when He returns.

In addition, the verse challenges us to consider the impact of our spiritual sleepiness on others. The Bible teaches that we are called to be a light to the world, to reflect God's love, truth, and grace to those around us. However, when we allow ourselves to become spiritually sleepy, our light grows dim, and we become less effective in our witness to others. A life given to drink and spiritual sleepiness not only affects our own relationship with God but also has a ripple effect on those around us—our families, our friends, our communities. The verse from 1 Thessalonians 5:7 reminds us that our spiritual vigilance is not just for our own sake, but for the sake of others as well. By staying awake, sober-minded, and spiritually alert, we can be a source of encouragement, guidance, and support to others, helping them to avoid the pitfalls of spiritual sleepiness and to remain strong in their faith.

Moreover, the verse calls us to a higher standard of living, one that is marked by self-control, discipline, and a focus on eternal values. The Bible teaches that the Christian life is a journey, one that requires perseverance, dedication, and a constant pursuit of holiness. To achieve this, we must remain spiritually awake, resisting the temptations that seek to pull us away from our path. Alcohol, particularly when abused, represents one of these temptations, luring us into a state of spiritual sleepiness where we become complacent, unmotivated, and disconnected from our faith. The verse from 1 Thessalonians 5:7 challenges us to rise above this, to live with a sense of purpose and urgency, and to remain vigilant in our walk with God. By doing so, we can avoid the dangers of spiritual sleepiness and instead live a life that is fully engaged, fully awake, and fully aligned with God's will.

In conclusion, 1 Thessalonians 5:7 offers a powerful and sobering warning about the dangers of spiritual sleepiness that often accompany indulgence in alcohol. The verse highlights the deep connection between physical drunkenness and spiritual unawareness, painting a vivid picture of the dangers that come with allowing oneself to be lulled into a state of complacency and unpreparedness. This kind of sleepiness is particularly dangerous because it goes unnoticed, gradually leading a person away from their faith, from God, and from the spiritual vigilance required to navigate the challenges and trials of life. The verse serves as a call to wakefulness, urging believers to stay alert, sober-minded, and fully engaged in their walk with God. It challenges us to resist the temptations of alcohol and the worldly attitudes that promote it, to live in the light, and to be a source of encouragement and support to others. By heeding this warning, we can avoid the pitfalls of spiritual sleepiness, remain strong in our faith, and live a life that is fully awake, fully alive, and fully dedicated to the service of God and His kingdom. The call is to turn away from the temporary pleasures that lead to sleepiness, to seek the wisdom and guidance of God, and to live with a sense of purpose, urgency, and readiness for the return of Christ.

Chapter 25 – The Skewed Judgment

Proverbs 31:4-5, "It is not for kings, O Lemuel, it is not for kings to drink wine; nor for princes strong drink: Lest they drink, and forget the law, and pervert the judgment of any of the afflicted," provides a profound and timeless warning about the dangers of alcohol, particularly for those in positions of leadership and responsibility. This passage is a direct admonition to King Lemuel, urging him to avoid the pitfalls of alcohol because of its ability to impair judgment and lead to poor decisions, especially when it comes to the governance and care of others. The phrase "skewed judgment" perfectly encapsulates the core message of this scripture, which is that the consumption of alcohol can distort one's ability to think clearly, make wise decisions, and uphold justice. For a king, whose primary duties include making laws, ensuring justice, and protecting the well-being of the people, any impairment of judgment can have serious, far-reaching consequences. The warning here is not just about the personal effects of alcohol, but about the broader impact that a leader's poor decisions can have on the lives of those who depend on them.

The verse begins by emphasizing that it is not fitting for kings or princes—those who hold positions of authority and power—to indulge in wine or strong drink. This is not merely a suggestion, but a strong directive, highlighting the unique responsibilities that come with leadership. A king or leader is expected to be a model of wisdom, integrity, and self-control, guiding their people with a clear mind and a steady hand. When a leader drinks alcohol, especially to excess, they compromise their ability to fulfill these responsibilities. Alcohol clouds the mind, dulls the senses, and impairs one's ability to think critically and act decisively. For a leader, whose decisions affect not just themselves but the entire community, this kind of impairment can lead to disastrous outcomes. The verse from Proverbs 31:4-5 serves as a powerful reminder that those in leadership must be especially vigilant about avoiding anything that could compromise their judgment or lead them to make decisions that are not in the best interest of those they serve.

The phrase "lest they drink, and forget the law" underscores the serious consequences of alcohol consumption for those in positions of authority. The law, in this context, represents not only the legal codes that govern society but also the moral and ethical principles that should guide a leader's actions. A leader who forgets the law is one who becomes disconnected from the very foundation of justice and fairness, leading to decisions that are arbitrary, unjust, and potentially harmful to the vulnerable and oppressed. Alcohol has the insidious ability to cause people to lose sight of their values, to ignore their responsibilities, and to act in ways that are contrary to their duties and commitments. For a king or leader, forgetting the law can mean failing to protect the rights of the afflicted, neglecting the needs of the poor, and allowing injustice to flourish. The verse warns that the consumption of alcohol can lead to a dangerous erosion of the principles that should guide a leader's actions, resulting in skewed judgment and poor decision-making.

Moreover, the verse highlights the specific danger of "perverting the judgment of any of the afflicted." This phrase speaks to the profound impact that a leader's impaired judgment can have on the most vulnerable members of society. The afflicted, in this context, refers to those who are suffering, oppressed, or in need of protection and support. It is the duty of a king or leader to ensure that these individuals receive justice and are treated with fairness and compassion. However, when a leader indulges in alcohol, their ability to fulfill this duty is compromised. Their judgment becomes skewed, and they may make decisions that are unfair, unjust, or harmful to those who are most in need of their protection. This is one of the most serious consequences of alcohol consumption for leaders: the potential to cause harm to those who are already vulnerable and to perpetuate injustice rather than preventing it. The verse from Proverbs 31:4-5 serves as a stark reminder that leaders must remain sober and clear-headed, always mindful of their responsibility to protect and serve the afflicted.

The concept of skewed judgment also extends to the broader implications of leadership in any context, not just for kings and princes. Whether in government, business, education, or even within a family, those in positions of authority are entrusted with the responsibility of making decisions that impact the lives of others. Alcohol, with its ability to impair cognitive function and judgment, poses a significant risk to anyone in a leadership role. A leader who is under the influence of alcohol is more likely to make impulsive decisions, to overlook important details, and to act based on emotion rather than reason. This can lead to a cascade of poor decisions that affect not only the leader but also those who rely on them for guidance and support. The verse from Proverbs serves as a timeless warning that the responsibilities of leadership require a clear mind and sound judgment, and that indulging in alcohol can seriously undermine a leader's ability to fulfill these responsibilities effectively.

Furthermore, the verse challenges us to consider the broader moral and ethical implications of alcohol consumption, particularly in relation to our responsibilities to others. The Bible consistently teaches that we are to love our neighbors, to act justly, and to care for the vulnerable. When we allow alcohol to impair our judgment, we are at risk of failing to live up to these moral obligations. Skewed judgment leads to actions that are not only harmful to ourselves but also to others, particularly those who are most in need of our protection and support. The verse from Proverbs 31:4-5 reminds us that our actions, especially those influenced by alcohol, have consequences that extend beyond our own lives. As such, it calls us to exercise self-control, to avoid anything that could impair our ability to make just and fair decisions, and to remain vigilant in our commitment to upholding the principles of justice and compassion.

The verse also speaks to the importance of self-discipline and restraint in leadership. A leader who indulges in alcohol is one who lacks the self-discipline necessary to maintain a clear mind and to make wise decisions. The Bible teaches that self-control is a fruit of the Spirit, a quality that is essential for living a life that is pleasing to God and beneficial to others. When a leader lacks self-control, they are more likely to give in to the temptations of alcohol and other vices, leading to a life that is marked by poor decisions, damaged relationships, and ultimately, a failure to fulfill their God-given responsibilities. The verse from Proverbs 31:4-5 serves as a call to cultivate self-discipline, to resist the pull of alcohol, and to remain focused on the duties and responsibilities that come with leadership. By doing so, leaders can avoid the pitfalls of skewed judgment and instead make decisions that are just, fair, and in the best interest of those they serve.

Additionally, the verse challenges us to reflect on the cultural attitudes toward alcohol and its consumption, particularly in relation to leadership. In many cultures, alcohol is often associated with celebration, relaxation, and socialization. However, the Bible warns that while alcohol may have its place, it must be approached with caution, especially by those in positions of authority. The verse from Proverbs 31:4-5 reminds us that leadership is a serious responsibility that requires a clear mind, sound judgment, and a commitment to justice. When cultural norms encourage or even glorify the consumption of alcohol, it becomes all the more important for leaders to exercise discernment and to avoid allowing these norms to influence their decisions. The verse calls for a counter-cultural approach to leadership, one that prioritizes the well-being of others over personal indulgence, and that recognizes the far-reaching consequences of impaired judgment.

Moreover, the verse serves as a reminder that the true strength of a leader lies not in their ability to indulge in alcohol or to enjoy the pleasures of life, but in their ability to make wise, just, and fair decisions that benefit those they lead. The Bible teaches that true leadership is marked by humility, wisdom, and a commitment to serving others. A leader who allows alcohol to impair their judgment is one who is putting their own desires above the needs of their people, and who is failing to live up to the high standards of leadership that God calls for. The verse from Proverbs 31:4-5 challenges leaders to seek strength not in alcohol, but in their relationship with God, in their commitment to justice, and in their dedication to serving others. By doing so, they can avoid the dangers of skewed judgment and instead lead with integrity, wisdom, and compassion.

In conclusion, Proverbs 31:4-5 offers a powerful and timeless warning about the dangers of alcohol, particularly for those in positions of leadership. The verse highlights the profound impact that alcohol can have on a leader's judgment, leading to poor decisions, a disregard for the law, and a failure to protect the vulnerable. The phrase "skewed judgment" encapsulates the core message of the verse, which is that the consumption of alcohol can distort one's ability to think clearly, make wise decisions, and uphold justice. The verse serves as a call to leaders to exercise self-discipline, to avoid the pitfalls of alcohol, and to remain vigilant in their commitment to justice and fairness. It also challenges us to reflect on the broader cultural attitudes toward alcohol and to recognize the importance of maintaining a clear mind and sound judgment, particularly in roles of authority. By heeding this warning, leaders can avoid the dangers of skewed judgment, make decisions that are just and fair, and fulfill their God-given responsibilities with integrity and wisdom. The call is to turn away from the temporary pleasures of alcohol, to seek strength and guidance in God, and to lead with a focus on justice, compassion, and the well-being of those they serve.

Conclusion

As we reach the conclusion of *Stumbling in the Dark - The Dangers of Alcohol in Scripture*, it's clear that the Bible's warnings about alcohol are as relevant today as they were in ancient times. Throughout this book, we've explored how alcohol can cloud judgment, lead to poor decisions, and create a path of destruction not just for the individual but also for those around them. The Scriptures have shown us that alcohol, when misused, has the power to pull us away from the clarity and wisdom that God desires for our lives. It can lead to spiritual sleepiness, causing us to lose our focus on what truly matters and dulling our sensitivity to God's guidance. The stories and teachings we've examined serve as powerful reminders that while alcohol may offer temporary relief or pleasure, its consequences can be long-lasting and devastating. The Bible does not condemn alcohol outright, but it does call us to be wise and vigilant, to recognize the dangers that come with overindulgence, and to avoid letting anything take control over us that could lead us away from God's path. As we reflect on these lessons, it's important to remember that living a life of sobriety—both in the literal sense and in the spiritual sense—is about more than just avoiding the pitfalls of alcohol. It's about staying alert, keeping our hearts and minds clear, and being fully present in our walk with God. By understanding the dangers of alcohol through the lens of Scripture, we can make better choices that protect our physical health, our relationships, and our spiritual well-being. This book has not only been a journey through the warnings and consequences of alcohol but also an invitation to live in the light, where God's wisdom guides our every step. As you close these pages, I encourage you to take these lessons to heart, to be mindful of the choices you make, and to seek the fullness of life that comes from walking closely with God, free from the darkness that alcohol can bring. May you find strength in His Word, wisdom in His teachings, and peace in living a life that honors Him in all things.

Don't miss out!

Visit the website below and you can sign up to receive emails whenever Joshua Rhoades publishes a new book. There's no charge and no obligation.

https://books2read.com/r/B-A-AJLBB-QEHYE

BOOKS2READ

Connecting independent readers to independent writers.

Did you love *Stumbling in the Dark - The Dangers of Alcohol*? Then you should read *Flee Fornication: The Plea For Purity*[1] by Joshua Rhoades!

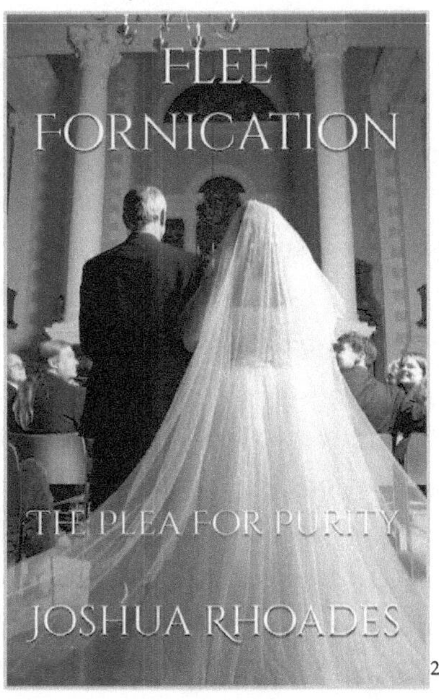

[2]

"Flee Fornication - The Plea For Purity" is an essential read for anyone grappling with the challenges of maintaining sexual purity in a world that often glorifies the opposite. This book dives deep into the spiritual and moral pitfalls that can ensnare individuals, drawing them away from a life of purity and toward a path of destruction. It doesn't shy away from addressing the real temptations and struggles that believers face daily, offering a candid look at the consequences of fornication, both spiritually and physically. Grounded in Scripture, calls readers to heed the biblical plea found in 1 Corinthians 6:18, where the Apostle Paul urges, "Flee fornication. Every sin that a man doeth is without

---

1. https://books2read.com/u/3GLqln

2. https://books2read.com/u/3GLqln

the body; but he that committeth fornication sinneth against his own body." This verse serves as the cornerstone of the book, emphasizing the severe spiritual implications of sexual immorality. From the story of Joseph fleeing Potiphar's wife to David's tragic fall with Bathsheba, the book illustrates the importance of vigilance and the devastating consequences of yielding to temptation. It also highlights the power of God's grace and the importance of repentance and restoration for those who have stumbled. The book doesn't just focus on the negative aspects but also provides uplifting encouragement on how to live a life of purity, including practical steps such as setting boundaries, avoiding compromising situations, and seeking accountability. The author stresses that purity is not just about saying "no" to sin but about saying "yes" to a deeper relationship with God. By committing to purity, believers can experience a closer walk with God, free from the guilt and shame that sexual sin brings. The book also considers the role of the Holy Spirit in empowering believers to overcome temptation and live a life that honors God. It is a call to action for those who desire to live a life that reflects the holiness of God, reminding readers that their bodies are temples of the Holy Spirit, and they are called to honor God with their bodies (1 Corinthians 6:19-20). "Flee Fornication - The Plea For Purity" is a powerful and timely message for a generation bombarded with sexual temptation, offering hope, healing, and a path to victory through Christ.